What people are saying about
The Peace Equation

Peace! *Anybody want it? Anybody need it? Anybody desperate for it? Do I sense many answering a resounding "YES!" to these questions?*

Well, I exhort you to get a copy of Steve's book and find the essence of the PEACE EQUATION, which the author has found and shares in his short, but powerful, book. I personally believe you'll be blessed, even if the blessing, like it did for Jacob, comes with a wrestling match with God. **Rev. Bill Berry, Ph.D. Director, Battle Plan Ministries**

… A definite five star if not more. Has come to me at the right time in my life and has blessed me beyond words.
Robin Bee Owens, *Three Children and a Blessing*

I love books [that] bleed real...that wrestle with a loving God in the midst of the realities of life that you could never imagine and definitely did not sign up for...The Peace Equation is the journey of a committed Christian father, husband, and church elder/leader who is attempting to "not be anxious" when life as you know it is unraveling. The Peace Equation offers us the supernatural peace and love of God that enables our faltering faith to not just survive but to truly thrive! **Dr. Ernie Frey, Pastor, Missionary, Global Discipleship Movement Leader**

THE PEACE EQUATION

God's process to help you overcome anxiety – and maintain your sanity – in a crisis.

Written by
Steve Gibbs

Published by
Sacred Grounds
(books on a higher order from Inknbeans Press)
© 2016

Cover by Evonne, the art elf
© 2016 Steve Gibbs and Sacred Grounds (books on a higher order from Inknbeans Press)

ISBN-13: 978-0692627945 (Sacred Grounds)

ISBN-10: 0692627944

The Peace Equation

Contents

Dedication

The two most important women in my life...

Joyce Halbrook Gibbs. My mother did not grow up in a religious family and she married very young – 15. Yet, she felt it was important that her children go to church, so she took us every week. She accepted Jesus Christ as her Lord and Savior while still a young mom. Over time, all six of her kids became believers, too. Eventually my dad got saved. There will be a wonderful reunion in heaven one day where we all can properly thank her.

Tracy Phifer Gibbs. My wife brings balance to our marriage. She is always encouraging, willing to help, happy, wise, patient... I am usually the opposite of those. Thirty-three years of marriage is not half enough. She is a person of great value and everyone knows it. And she remains the prettiest girl in Memphis, Tennessee.

Acknowledgements

This book would never have happened without the help of these individuals:

Dr. Bill Bellican. Our counselor through many hard days. Your contributions were extremely valuable as I was writing this book.

Dr. Philip C. Eyster. My friend, advisor and editor. I've learned much from you, brother.

Rev. John Willis. A great role model and prayer partner. You are my hot line in times of trouble.

Maaijo Lowe. You were the answer to a prayer and you fulfilled a dream. You are also perhaps the nicest person with whom I have ever worked.

To the families mentioned in this book who have suffered loss and heartbreak, thank you for sharing your powerful stories as an inspiration to others.

Preface

God gave me a revelation in the wee hours one morning when my mind was churning with all of the crises that were tormenting me; my failure in business, my failure in friendship, my failure as a parent, my failure as a church leader... The demons took turns lashing me, variously bringing these issues to mind, rehashing the details of each situation and providing images of the possible outcomes, all of which were horrible. My anxiety attack started slowly at first, and then picked up momentum until I was in near panic. With clinched fists and teeth, I begged God in my thoughts for His miraculous intervention in my life. Save me, oh God! I am drowning, just like Peter when his faith floundered and he began sinking into the Sea of Galilee. This night was like so many others before; sweating, tossing, turning, fear upon fear – I was even worried how my lack of sleep would affect my day tomorrow. I would be exhausted. I was already exhausted!

God's life preserver came in the form of a Scripture verse, or rather, just a sentence fragment from Scripture; "peace that surpasses all understanding." Where did that verse come from? It had been floating around in my brain for a day or so. It was a verse tucked away in my memory like a knickknack in our linen closet. I couldn't remember where it came from and I didn't know exactly what it meant. It was a verse I had thought of many times before in moments of mental anguish and strife, but its meaning was abstract. What exactly is the peace of God? If I am a believer and follower of Jesus, why don't I have it? My mind was in chaos and my anxiety at DEFCON one! I seriously doubted my sanity. I realized how people might contemplate suicide.

As it turns out, that bit of scripture God planted in my mind is from Philippians 4. In the first century the followers of Jesus Christ didn't have Xanax, Valium or Pharrell Williams. They had the Apostle Paul to remind them that God is the ultimate source of peace and happiness.

"Rejoice in the Lord always; again I will say, rejoice. Let your reasonableness be known to everyone. The Lord is at hand; do not be anxious about anything, but in everything by prayer and supplication with thanksgiving let your requests be made known to God. And the peace of God, which surpasses all

understanding, will guard your hearts and your minds in Christ Jesus. *(Philippians 4:4-7, ESV)*

The answer to my anxiety and stress problem was somehow connected to that passage. But why was it not true for me? I've been reasonable with everyone, tried not to be anxious and offered my prayer requests with thanksgiving to the Lord. But despite following the instructions found in Philippians 4, I could only achieve brief moments of peace and would soon swoon back into anxiety and fear. As I contemplated my own peace problem, it occurred to me that there were probably many other Christians who struggle with the same internal conflict created by Philippians 4 – they believe in Jesus but can't escape worry and stress. Philippians 4 hangs over them like a piñata filled with happiness, but they are somehow blindfolded and cannot see it. If I could crack open the secret of Philippians 4, maybe I could help others crack it open, too.

Laying there in the dark, I reviewed my own spiritual journey over the previous 36 months. As I did, the Holy Spirit began to reveal the *process* I had gone through. Like planks on a rope bridge, I saw my progression – the spiritual battle, the mental battle, my experiences as the father of an addicted daughter, the role of Godly people in my life, the extreme value of Scripture, worship and counseling. God revealed to me that these planks – this process – create the pathway from chaos to peace, and each step is necessary to achieve a genuine, enduring peace. I spent the next two hours typing the outline for this book.

Just as He had in previous times of great spiritual struggle, the Holy Spirit came at just the right time to lift me from the quicksand that was consuming me. Suddenly there was clarity as God revealed light in my darkened soul. The warm embrace of God's arm was around my shoulder, holding me up and urging me forward. Extreme anxiety gave way to peace... and relief. I had a new perspective on my pain, something that God revealed to me as His "Peace Equation," a process that only He can lead you through. It's there, in His Word, and Philippians 4 began my discovery process. Thank you, oh Heavenly Father! You have not forsaken me.

THE PEACE EQUATION

God's process to help you overcome anxiety – and maintain your sanity – in a crisis.

(written on the day my daughter Jordan moved to college)

August 25, 2006

My dearest Lefty,

Well, the time I have dreaded has come. When you were a little bitty girl with curly hair and big blue eyes I thought about the day you would go to college. I choked up at the thought. I can't believe that 18 years have gone by so quickly – the blink of an eye. You'll understand the swiftness of life when you have children.

You may not know it, but I have a little tradition of writing letters to your mother on big occasions. I wrote the first one on the day we were married. I thought it might be a nice thing to do with you, as well. For some time now I've been contemplating what I would write in this letter. I don't want it to be too gushy or sentimental, but there is some important stuff I want to tell you, stuff maybe I forgot to mention as you were growing up. You know, I've had only 18 years to communicate with you, and I think that's only about half enough time.

So, while I still have a chance, here are some of the things I think are important.

In no particular order...

- *Try to avoid using credit cards – debt is a very bad thing.*
- *Never pour water on a grease fire (I learned this one the hard way).*
- *Stay close with your sister and brother ALWAYS. They are the two people in the whole world who truly know who you are.*
- *Try to hang around with people who know Jesus personally.*
- *Driving fast causes more problems than it solves. Slow down.*
- *Doing nice things for people is the real secret to happiness.*
- *Smoking anything is extremely stupid. You are not stupid.*
- *Dogs are more fun that cats. Cats are more fun that rodents.*
- *God REALLY DOES have someone picked for you to marry. I believe this with all my heart. Pray that He will make the proper introduction at the right time. I will pray for the same thing.*
- *Get lots of exercise. It builds self-confidence and keeps you fit.*
- *"Having a lot in common" doesn't make a good husband. Look for someone who has the same values as you.*
- *Decide right away what are the things you truly value.*

- *Never, EVER drive after you have been drinking.*
- *Dance whenever possible. I didn't dance enough and that made your mother sad.*
- *Hard work is extremely important, but less important than following Christ.*
- *Talk to God every day. Don't just pray, talk to Him.*
- *Never look down on anybody, except those who are wealthy and arrogant.*
- *Never punch a door (I learned this one the hard way).*
- *Sex before marriage only makes life complicated and usually hurts everyone involved. If you think you're in love, wait.*
- *God is the best business partner you can ever have.*
- *Always do what is right. This will gratify some and astonish the rest (Will Rodgers).*
- *Think of others as more important than yourself. That's Bible advice.*
- *Don't waste years of your life on drugs and self-gratification. Living for God is the only thing that brings real fulfillment (I learned this one the hard way).*
- *It's the most wonderful thing when your spouse is your best friend.*
- *Go to Paris at least once in your life.*

- *Sing with your children. I don't think we sang enough.*
- *Tell the people you love "I love you." You can never say that enough.*

Okay, I guess you're on your own now. Go make good decisions. Please come home when you can – remember that you are the only one in the whole Gibbs clan who has eyes exactly the color of my mother's. I have to see those eyes every now and then. You can never do anything that will make me love you less. Lefty, to me you are the moon and all the stars rolled into one.

With all my love,

Dad

Introduction Life's a game but sometimes it's not much fun.

Some say "life is a journey," but that seems really cliché. To me, life is more like a board game. The "Game of Life" you might say, if that isn't copyright infringement. A roll of the dice determines what will happen next. From our human perspective, life seems random, as if dictated by chance. As a Christian (I prefer to call myself a "follower of Jesus"), I know that God holds all the days and events of my existence, but to me, standing here on the game board, there's no way to know what is coming next. It depends on the dice. Where will I land on the board? Will I go back three spaces, lose a turn, advance to Boardwalk, take a ride on the Reading, or go directly to jail? God may know the future and have a plan for my life, but what happens tomorrow or next year will be a surprise to me, and that creates stress. We just have to take life as it happens and hang on to the "get out of jail FREE" card that Christ has provided to those who believe.

I've never been to jail, but I have been in prison, the prison of anxiety and fear. Anxiety, fear, stress and worry... they all feel like jail. Heavy anxiety, the kind that paralyzes you, is like physical pain. It is like a constant dull ache. It distracts you, disables and weakens you. You may labor to breathe. You sometimes can think of nothing but your problems, and that makes work and home life difficult and can make those around you miserable. After all, who wants to live or work with a grouchy, gloomy jackass? And anxiety is self-perpetuating; it leads to depression, which makes you worry that you have a mental illness, which makes you more depressed. It goes on and on. Meanwhile, if you are a Christian, you pray. You ask God to change your circumstances, or maybe you pray for greater faith to get through the turmoil, or you pray that the Father will forgive your lack of faith. The very thought that you lack faith makes you depressed, so the cycle continues. It's a merry-go-round of ugly gargoyles and funeral music that you want to get off, but you can't.

Unless you are extremely self-absorbed, you understand that everyone has problems. I have big problems, but I don't have to look very hard to find others who have problems bigger than mine. For every lost job or car wreck there is someone else who finds a lump in their breast or drugs in their kid's pocket. It's a game of poker where everyone keeps upping the ante with worse bad news. If you have ever listened to prayer requests in a Sunday School class you understand what I mean. It seems that each person in the circle has a life-crushing issue, or knows someone who has one. Okay, life is hard, I get it. But someone else's worries don't make mine any easier. I still have overwhelming financial problems even if your wife leaves you for another man. Misery loves company, but the whole crowd is still miserable. Do someone else's problems put mine in perspective? Maybe, but I'm still filled with anguish and worry. I'm still on the gargoyle merry-go-round.

According to the Anxiety and Depression Association of America, anxiety disorders are the most common form of mental illness in the United States, affecting some 40 million adults.[1] The ADAA also notes that anxiety and depression cost the U.S. a staggering $42 billion annually. The very fact that there *is* an Anxiety and Depression Association is enough to make you reach for an Ativan. The Centers for Disease Control (CDC) defines depression as a "depressed or sad mood, diminished interest in activities which used to be pleasurable... inappropriate guilt, difficulties concentrating, as well as recurrent thoughts of death.[2]" Sound familiar? The CDC also notes that major depression frequently goes unrecognized and untreated, and that it can "foster tragic consequences such as suicide and impaired personal relationships." No question, depression is serious business. Of course, not everyone suffers from clinical depression;

7

in many cases, people are dealing with the anxiety and stress that result from difficult life challenges. The National Institute for Mental Health reports that 18 percent of adults, almost one-in-five, have anxiety disorders.[3] More than two-thirds of Americans, about 69 percent, say they experience physical symptoms of stress, according to the American Psychological Association[4]. Clearly, a lot of people are dealing with either mild or severe mental health issues, either long term or temporarily. Many have clinical problems that require psychiatric care and medication, while others are dealing with emotional issues created by serious real-life problems such as divorce, chronic illness, habitual drug abuse, bullying or other circumstances. These problems can be very weighty and take months or years to resolve, if they are ever resolved. Some problems, like narcotic addiction or the death of a loved one are "life sentences." We may spend the rest of our lives learning to cope with the problem and battling to keep it from overshadowing the good stuff that happens, like graduations, weddings, grandkids and seeing others become Jesus followers.

Depression and anxiety may be a problem for "ordinary folk," but what about us Christians? Aren't we supposed to be immune to worry?

The Beatles sang, "When I find myself in times of trouble, Mother Mary comes to me, speaking words of wisdom, let it be." Great lyrics for a song, but

8

not scripturally sound or useful in an actual emergency. Christians know that in times of trouble, we can turn to the Lord for comfort, truth and, perhaps most importantly, wisdom. What should you, as a believer in Jesus Christ, do when your world is falling apart? The answer: pray, read the Word, give thanks and worship. You also may seek counseling, either to help solve the actual problem (debt, grief, divorce, etc.) or deal with the related spiritual issue (losing your faith or, in my case, being stressed and anxious). People who are knowledgeable of Scripture know that the Bible offers a great deal of advice about some of life's biggest problems – marital infidelity, financial woes, the death of a loved one, serious illness, business dealings, disagreements among believers, social and political issues... the list is long. Most big problems, but not all, are in some way addressed in Scripture. The passages listed in this book represent only part of what God has to say about these issues; a complete understanding of God's counsel requires great study and meditation on His Word.

It is also important to note that some of life's challenges are inexplicable this side of heaven. As James Dobson wrote in *When God Doesn't Make Sense*, "Trying to analyze (God's) omnipotence is like an amoeba attempting to comprehend the behavior of man.[5]" The New Living Translation of Ecclesiastes 11:5 puts it this way:

"Just as you cannot understand the path of the wind or the mystery of a tiny baby growing in its mother's womb, so you cannot understand the activity of God, who does all things."

Mere humans cannot fathom God's complex plan for humanity, but our loving Father will explain it all when we are with Him in eternity. For now, we have to trust His love and wisdom.

That being said, as a human, I don't like the thought of living with grief, worry and despair for several decades until I'm in heaven. Emotional pain is painful and a heavy burden to carry. God wants us to have mental and spiritual peace in all circumstances and at all times (*"Now may the Lord of peace himself give you peace at all times in every way."* 2 Thessalonians 3:16). I would prefer to live happily, or at least peacefully, without a war going on in my mind. So, when exceptionally bad things happen in my life, I have immediately turned to God (well, immediately after a brief period of shock and panic), because I have read in the Bible about God's *peace that surpasses all understanding*. I want the fear and anxiety to go away. I want relief from the stress. I want mental, emotional and spiritual peace. Sometimes after much prayer and Scripture reading I have experienced a brief release of tension, maybe one could even describe it as peace.

The Lord does speak to me through the Bible and I find genuine comfort there, but the relief has typically been temporary, it is not a peace that surpasses all understanding. Most often, it is only a pause from the punishment, like the break boxers get between rounds. When it's over, the pummeling resumes, and I have the bruises and red eyes to prove it.

I know God's Word is true, so why don't I find genuine peace in the midst of troubles? Why do I hurt so badly? Why have I, after several significant trials over the past three years, begun to fear the future? Am I wrong about the whole "God thing?" Is He really a loving Father or an unemotional deity who is ambivalent about my suffering? Does he even really exist? If you take enough shots to the heart, you begin to think such thoughts.

These emotions may be familiar to you, too. As an elder in my church, I speak with many genuine, born-again believers who are battling stress, anxiety and fear. The triggers are often serious illness, marital problems, job loss or a family crisis such as drug addiction. They sincerely desire the peace that only God can provide, but it is often elusive, or may seem impossible to attain. What about the parents who bury a child or the sweet saint who has suffered from severe arthritis for 20 years and has little hope of ever living pain free? Can they ever have peace that surpasses all understanding? Their emotional stress

11

and depression may never go away. Why? Is it a faith issue? Do they not "believe" enough? What are they missing that is preventing them from having God's unshakable peace?

For someone who is going through a difficult time AND is prone to depression, this is a depressing revelation. I began to fear that the big problems in my life might never get better. Maybe you fear the same thing. Based on my family history, I have about 20 more years of life ahead. The thought of living 20 more years under a dark cloud is a real bummer. Like Jimmy Stewart, I wanted "A Wonderful Life," but I felt more like Sean Penn in "Dead Man Walking." As a follower of Jesus, suicide was not an option; I wouldn't want to hurt my Christian testimony by blowing my brains out! I underwent Christian counseling, but after a few sessions I felt I stopped making progress. I have sometimes poured out my heart to close friends who could provide advice, and to my poor wife, Tracy, who had to listen to hours of my moaning and psychological self-analysis. She became a true shoulder for my tears, but I wore her out with my constant whining and complaining. What kind of man has to lean on his wife constantly for emotional support? At the end of the day I had only once place to go: back to God.

More Scripture reading, more prayer, more Christian books, more self-loathing... does any of this sound familiar to you? Satan had me in a death spiral of pity and pain. It turns out that the devil really is like a lion, seeking whom he may devour (I Peter 5:8). I understand that verse in a whole new way now. I was being eaten alive, from the inside out. How did I react to the anxiety and pressure? I quit a lucrative job and deserted a good friend in an attempt to relieve some of the stress I felt. I seriously considered resigning as an elder. I would have resigned as a husband and father, but my wife wouldn't let me. I actually felt I was teetering on the edge of insanity. To me, the peace that surpasses all understanding was a concept, not a reality. It must be some after-life peace that comes in heaven, because life on this earth was a living hell.

Fortunately, Jesus did not leave us without help in life's most difficult circumstances. The Holy Spirit, whom Jesus referred to as "The Comforter," is an incredible resource for the believer. The role of The Comforter is not just to provide physical and spiritual comfort, like a cozy afghan on a chilly day. The Holy Spirit also leads us into all truth, and the truth is that the peace that surpasses all understanding is available to every Christ follower, no matter how painful your situation. You may think, "my pain is too deep, my loss too great to ever have real peace again." That is simply untrue; it has to be, because God promises genuine peace if we align ourselves with His perspective and purpose. But don't think this type of peace comes easily or cheap. God's peace requires us to go through a *process* that builds our faith, creates confidence in God's promises, and gives us a heavenly perspective. The process involves several necessary steps that can turn your anxiety, stress and fear into unsurpassed peace. Be aware, however, that your process may require time and repeated lessons from the Master Teacher. For me, it took more than three years of advanced study in God's classroom of life, and even now stress and anxiety are sometimes on the edge of my consciousness. But peace HAS prevailed, and I thank God for the process.

Many people – perhaps you are one of them – are in the prison of stress, anxiety, grief and fear, and they look to God for freedom. If you are one of these prisoners, you must understand that the Father can only help those who have accepted Jesus Christ as their Lord and Savior. Becoming a disciple of Jesus is the prerequisite for freedom from these terrible emotional pains. The promises He makes in Scripture only work for Jesus followers; others must rely on their own strength to overcome emotional pain. Often the pain is overwhelming and insurmountable. However, for believers there is hope and a process that God uses to spring us from the prison that comes from great anxiety. I call the process The Peace Equation.

There are usually times in every believer's life where God suddenly, maybe even abruptly shows up. Most often it is when we, like Peter, begin to sink and cry out, "Lord, save me!" In the game of life, you sometimes land on an undesirable space: Your marriage is over. Your loved one is dying. You are facing bankruptcy. The issue may seem unbearable in the moment as you realize you are about to lose something of great value, something you love. That was me during the years 2011 through 2013. The accumulation of bad news became more than I could bear. I cried out to God and He revealed to me His method – His equation – for dealing with stress. The rest of this book is His story.

(Most of the "Letters to Lefty" in this book were written while Jordan, our oldest child, was in treatment for addiction. It was my way of encouraging her. Lefty is our nickname for Jordan.)

August 26, 2011

Dear Lefty:

The day I write this, August 26, is the anniversary of my dad's birth. He would have been 93 today. He was only 57 when he passed away. Your Aunt Janis and I remarked at the time that he had lived a "full life." I'll be 55 soon. My perspective on age 57 is totally different now!

It is a pity that none of my children had a chance to know my dad. He was a larger guy than I am, in almost every way. He was nearly six-feet tall, wore horn-rimmed glasses most of his life (his eyesight was terrible, so you can "thank" him) and in his later years he had silver hair which he wore combed straight back. He was thick-bodied with an olive sort of complexion. My mother said that as a young man he was the most handsome boy in her school "by far." He was quite an athlete, too. Your Mammaw was honored that he took an interest in her and she fell for him immediately. He was 18 and she was 15.

16

My dad was generally quiet and contemplative, and he was respected by our friends and neighbors. He was considered by everyone to be fair and honest in all his dealings. His forthrightness is a trait all his children possess. In his conversations with us he seldom mentioned honesty and integrity, but we <u>knew</u> that being dishonest was the worst possible thing a person could do. I've told a lie or two in my lifetime, and when I did, I had the disapproving image of my dad in the back of my mind.

Before he became a Christian at age 54, he was antagonistic about church and resentful when our preacher, John Kimbrell, would stop by. However, my mother's persistence and many years of prayer paid off. My dad was baptized in the Arkansas River in 1972. We had a flat tire on the way home and he had to change it, soaking wet.

The last real conversation I had with my dad was exactly six days before he died. He was in the hospital in Little Rock suffering from cancer and I had come from Conway, where I was in college at the time. It was a Saturday night and it was just he and I. From his hospital window we could see the lights of War Memorial Stadium where the Razorbacks were playing their season-opening game. We talked about football and school. He said, "Make sure you work hard and finish college." It went unsaid that this was his dying wish for me.

17

On September 12, 1975, Oliver Harold Gibbs went to be with the Lord. I imagine he has enjoyed seeing the lives of his children and grandchildren unfold over the years.

I loved my dad and still do. When he died, someone told me, "you will think about your father every day of your life." I have.

Love,

Dad

Chapter 1 Peace of mind (and how I lost it)

"Be sober-minded; be watchful. Your adversary the devil prowls around like a roaring lion, seeking someone to devour." 1 Peter 5:8

Life is what happens when you are making other plans. John Lennon wrote that in a song; I quote The Beatles a lot to mask my weak literary background. In July of 2011, we were making plans. It was Saturday, just two days until the Fourth of July, which is a pretty big day for my family and neighbors. We have a big outdoor picnic in our cul-de-sac and afterward set off fireworks, which is technically prohibited in our town but winked at by the local police. Over the years the fireworks show has become something of a good-natured competition among the families who live here. Many of our kids have grown up together, so it is a shared memory. Great stuff.

The previous 18 months had been a bit of an emotional roller coaster for our family. It began in 2010 with me being selected as an elder of my church, a large independent evangelical church with 3,000 members. The role of elder is both an honor and a huge responsibility. Our church elders serve for life, sort of like the Supreme Court. My pastor at that time commented, "It will be both the best job and worst job you've ever had." He was right. I was humbled by my selection and dedicated myself to serve God as best I could for the rest of my days. Amen.

At almost the same time that I was selected as an elder, my wife, Tracy, was laid off by her company after 28 years. The layoff came just two months before she would have qualified for full retirement benefits, including lifetime healthcare coverage. No worries. As good Christians, we took the position that it was (A) God's will and (B) a blessing in disguise since Tracy had been eager to retire anyway. We decided to take the majority of her severance package and invest it in remodeling the kitchen. Tracy is an incredible cook with the gift of hospitality, and with a new kitchen, we rationalized, she could serve even more people. Side note, in one year she cooked and fed more than 500 college students who came to our home on Tuesday nights for Bible study – an average of about 25 students each time. She REALLY has the gift of hospitality! Anyhow, we hired a local contractor who we knew through our church to coordinate the project. It's a long story, but the end result was that he defrauded us of $15,000 and we were without a kitchen for four months. A disappointing setback, to be sure, but we again took it in stride (God's will, blessing in disguise). We tried to minister to the contractor and completely forgave him of his transgressions against us.

We were such STRONG Christians!

It was at about this time that our middle child, Haley, had a terrible car accident in which she ran off the highway and collided with a concrete wall. She was still trapped in the car when she called us – 150 miles away – from her mobile phone. She was crying and explained that she couldn't move her legs. You can only imagine the panic we experienced when the cops took the phone away as they extracted her from the car. Miraculously (thank you, Jesus!), she had no serious injuries. Nevertheless, it was the type of phone call no parent ever wants to get.

Mixing the good with the bad, our eldest daughter, Jordan, got married in October 2010 to a nice young man she met at work. Her wedding was an outdoor affair held on the most beautiful day in the history of Memphis, Tennessee. All our family and friends were there and we had a wonderful reception with dancing and wine. We even had a bagpiper, which was awesome. About five months later, in March 2011, we celebrated Tracy's 50th birthday with a party. I surprised her with a commissioned painting of our house done by one of her favorite local artists. It was so cool, and she loved it. We had survived the tribulations of a lost job, a serious car wreck and a home remodeling project gone bad and still loved the Lord with all our heart, mind and soul. My faith was unshakeable (I thought). I had spiritual and emotional peace despite the mess we had endured and I was looking forward to how God might use me in the future.

Enter the roaring lion, seeking someone to devour.

Our life plans were significantly altered on Saturday, July 2, 2011, about mid afternoon when I got a call from a close friend who owned a restaurant. He had been kind enough to hire my daughter, Jordan, as a server. A recent college graduate, Jordan was between jobs in a tough economy. She had jumped at the opportunity to wait tables and was doing an incredible job according to my friend, the owner. I was his spiritual mentor so getting a call on a Saturday made me think he had a problem and needed prayer. The conversation turned out much differently than I anticipated.

> Me: Hey Tom.
> Tom: I have some bad news.
> Me: What's up?
> Tom: I had to fire Jordan today.
> Me: What? Why?
> Tom: I caught her using drugs on the job.

Brief silence as I contemplated what to ask next.

Me: What kind of drugs?

Tom: Heroin. I'm sorry.

There are two reasons I'll never forget that conversation. The first reason is that I learned my precious daughter, the cum laude college graduate, the girl who had gone on mission trips and had participated in the church worship band, the girl who had scored a 31 on her ACT exam, was a heroin addict. The second reason I will always remember that call is because of Tom's last two words, "I'm sorry." I knew that Tom himself was recovering from substance abuse and had once run with a very rough crowd. He knew exactly what heroin could do to a person and the damage it would cause our entire family. In an instant I knew this was really bad news. His "I'm sorry" carried a world of meaning that we would come to understand over the next two years.

From that moment on, our "peace" was shattered. A whirlwind of activity followed. We immediately called Jordan's husband, who was not a drug user, and were told that Jordan was not there and he had no idea where she was. We went to their apartment to discuss our options with him and determine how best to help our daughter. In our conversation with him we began to learn of her secret life, a life that began in college with drug use that had

23

escalated in the usual way. We learned that he had helped her "dry out" even before they were married, and he assumed her heroin use had ended. But she had resumed at some point and was now shooting up, often multiple hits a day. We waited at her apartment that night for her to return. We had no idea if she would come home. At about 10 p.m., she walked in, unaware that we were there; we were hiding to make sure she would not run away if she saw us before entering. She was completely stoned. We stood in another room as she explained that she had been fired that day. We walked in to confront her, but in her state she was barely fazed by our presence. We chatted about helping her and our unwavering commitment, and we spoke of getting professional help as soon as possible. I prayed for her. We decided that both she and her husband should stay with us for the night so we could discuss our next move in the morning. Actually, we wanted to make sure she didn't run away into the streets of Memphis. My wife packed a bag for her and in doing so, found the syringes and other paraphernalia necessary for heroin use. The reality of the moment was overwhelming.

I slept on the sofa downstairs at our home that night, as Jordan, her husband and my wife slept upstairs – we had sent the other two children away for the night. I was sleeping downstairs to make sure she didn't try to sneak out in the middle of the night. From my vantage point on the couch, I could see into our foyer. On the wall, next to a coat closet, was a large family photo. The doorway to the foyer partially blocked my view and allowed me to see only Jordan in the photo and a portion of the closet door. The panels on the closet door that I could see formed a perfect cross, like the cross of Jesus. I lay there for hours looking at the image of my kid and the cross, weeping. Quietly, the Holy Spirit whispered in my ear, "I'm in this with you."

The next two years were a bitter, painful journey through addiction. Of course, the journey was much worse for my precious daughter, who struggled through the stages of withdrawal, guilt and feelings of hopelessness. She was kicked out of two treatment facilities and had to endure a time when we, her parents, had to turn our backs on her. We had learned a new vocabulary that included words like "enabling" and "detach with love." The low point for me was on my birthday in 2011 when Jordan was forced to call and inform us she had been expelled from her treatment facility – her second expulsion in five months – because she had broken the rules and used alcohol. "I'm sorry I had to tell you this on your birthday, Daddy." I spent most of that day lying on a couch in my office in the dark, completely broken. This was only one of many low points, times when we were in absolute despair worrying how it would all turn out.

My mind went to some horrible places. Addicts will do almost anything for a fix, including all types of criminal activity. Also, anyone familiar with heroin addiction knows that there are typically only three possible outcomes: recovery, jail or death. The odds for a happy outcome are not good.

Our daughter's addiction, by itself, was an incredible blow, but we were spiritually grounded and had counseling resources through our church, so we were able to find ways to hang on to our sanity and our faith in God. Our church has a Christian counselor on staff, Dr. Bill Bellican, who was able to steer us toward our first rehab experience. It was ultimately un-successful in treating our daughter, but this is not uncommon with serious addiction; addicts frequently go through multiple treatment facilities and halfway houses. Bill also provided excellent counseling to us and directed us to a support group, a local Nar-Anon family meeting where we met others who were also dealing with the addiction of loved ones. My wife and I also have incredibly supportive families who prayed and loved us in the worst of times. My middle daughter, Haley, who is so wonderful and generous, even moved back home for several months to help us pull through as a family.

If you have ever watched a boxing match you know that one punch rarely wins the fight. It is usually an accumulation of blows that wear down and sometimes knock out the opponent. Satan knows that he can't beat a dedicated Jesus follower with one punch, so he often combines his blows to achieve his desired effect, which is the destruction of the believer's faith. Such was our case. Satan had softened us up with the loss of my wife's job, my middle child's car wreck and the kitchen fiasco, as we came to call that incident. These were only preludes to his next attack, which was the roundhouse of my eldest daughter's addiction. This hit definitely staggered us, but we were still standing! He came next with a series of rabbit punches over the next two years and then a couple of powerful uppercuts that would nearly kill me.

This may seem like a silly problem, but when it is *your* child who is hurting, the problem is not silly at all. My son, Rainey, is an excellent athlete. Tall, lean, strong and fast, he grew up from Pee Wee Baseball to Little League to competitive ball to high school with the goal of becoming a star baseball player. I have always been objective about my kids and I can say, in all honesty, he has outstanding physical ability. He has a terrific arm, a good batting eye and, like Forrest Gump, he can run like the wind blows. According to one of his high school coaches, he was considered among the school's most promising players when he entered the ninth grade. This is at a large suburban high school with a long tradition of baseball excellence (the team has won numerous conference, regional and state championships). Rainey quickly established himself as a pitcher on the JV team and a regular in the outfield. We had dreams of him earning a college baseball scholarship.

What actually transpired over the next two years was extremely disappointing for Rainey and very sad for us, as it came at a time when we were grieving our daughter's addiction. Like many young athletes, Rainey is very competitive. He puts enormous pressure on himself to succeed. That kind of self-imposed pressure would be his undoing as a high school baseball player. He viewed every pitch as a referendum of his success or failure. When he was pitching, a bad first pitch might lead to a succession of terrible pitches and his being removed in the first inning. A called strike when he was batting would stress him to the point where he would tie himself up in knots on the next swing. A dropped ball in the outfield would ruin his entire day, whether in practice or a game. He simply could not relax and enjoy playing baseball. It was a condition we first saw in him as a Little Leaguer and one which got worse as he grew older. Both coaches and parents urged him to have fun and not put so much pressure on himself, but he couldn't do it. His anxiety affected his performance to the point he became very depressed. Meanwhile, he dropped so far down the bench that he rarely played, this despite his natural athletic ability. He quit baseball entering his junior year.

Sports are not as serious as drug addiction, but to see our son experience disappointment when he so desperately wanted to succeed was very painful. However, we saw this as God's will for his life. Rainey's a great student who now has time to devote to science projects and computer technology. He is a wonderful son who enjoys trout fishing with his old man. He's more relaxed these days and says he wants to major in computer science, which is great because I could use a good, and cheap, IT man.

As the addiction ordeal and my son's sports struggles were occurring, my personal world grew exponentially more stressful thanks to my job. In 2006, I became a partner in a marketing and communications firm based in St. Louis. I owned only a small percentage of the company, but I enjoyed significant authority due to the fact that the majority owner and founder was a close personal friend. He treated me as an equal partner, though he owned a 70 percent stake. We had an exciting, thriving business with some of America's biggest and best-known companies as clients. I frequently traveled the country on business trips and was responsible for million-dollar budgets. Then came the recession of 2008-09. During that time a key member of our ownership team quit to go to work for our biggest client, taking that business with her. Our other clients either scaled back their activities or "went dark." We survived, but barely. I didn't know until mid-2011 the extent we were hemorrhaging money. Our business manager at the time was disorganized and disinterested in helping us out of the mess. We eventually let her go, but by the time we realized the seriousness of our financial woes, we were on the razor's edge of bankruptcy. Every day for months we had to juggle funds to pay bills, often using our own personal credit cards to make ends meet. If our clients had known of our financial problems, we would likely have been fired immediately, so it was a constant dance to stay ahead of bill collectors and payroll. Our accounting system was virtually non-existent, so we were flying blind with almost zero knowledge of our actual financial situation beyond our bank balance on any particular day. Plus, we were always busy working on our clients' projects, which is more than a full-time job by itself. Add to that the workload associated with running a company: personnel, accounting, taxes, insurance, new business development... you get an idea of the stress that my partner and I were under. Twelve-hour workdays were often capped with either bad news regarding my daughter's addiction, my son's baseball disappointments or some other "normal" problem like a leaky roof, a dead car battery or some crisis at church. Life was piling trouble upon trouble and I did not have the luxury of concentrating on a single issue. Like a bad juggler I was trying to keep multiple bowling pins in the air, terrified that one would conk me on the head. I thought of the biblical characters Job and Jonah. Job had a multitude of miseries and became angry with God (more on that later). Jonah disobeyed God and tried to run away, only to bring about a storm on everyone around him. Was I, like Jonah, somehow the cause of these catastrophes? Maybe I should be tossed overboard and everything would get better. This type of thinking led me to quit my job in February 2014.

Guilt and depression ganged up on me. It was like suddenly being jumped by bad guys and getting into an unexpected fight. I don't know how it happened, but now the fists are flying and I have to defend myself. My head is on a swivel and my arms are up in self-defense. The punches sting and I feel the pain. But this is not a nightmare, it is reality. Will I survive?

I don't know exactly when my spiritual peace *completely* disappeared, but it was likely around February 2012. This was when we discovered Jordan's marriage was ending, while at the same time my business problems were at their worst. The culmination of all these issues had created a burden too heavy to bear; I was ready to give up. Over the next several months there would be brief periods of light when a passage of Scripture or praise song lifted my spirits, or God would lead some saint to provide a word of encouragement, but mostly I was consumed by gloom. I had no peace at all, and certainly not "peace that surpasses all understanding." Most of my days could be described as grim with intermittent periods of extreme anxiety and despair. I came to think that either God's promise was a lie or there was something seriously wrong in my relationship with Him.

August 30, 2011

Dear Lefty,

Following are several memories I have of you. Some are meaningful, some silly – they are just images of you stuck in my head.

- *"I WUV FIREMEN!" You were 3, I think. We were shooting a video to promote the Firemen's Calendar in Memphis. It "only" took 45 minutes and every ounce of cajoling we could muster to get you to say that one line. I think we had to promise you a new Barbie.*
- *Norma Jean. You were 5 or 6, I think, when you played "Norma Jean," the angel in the Christmas play. You stole the show. As I told mom at the time, "she may grow up to be an actor and win an Oscar, but I'll never be more proud of her than I am right now!"*
- *Remember when you got hit in the mouth by that softball? You were about 10. You immediately covered your mouth with your hands and I could see blood trickling through your fingers. Thought you'd lost your front teeth.*
- *The fountain in Disney World. We have this photo of you standing in a fountain somewhere in Disney World. It's the cutest*

photo you ever made – which is saying a lot because we have lots of cute photos of you.
- *You and Haley trudging off to the bus stop with those gigantic backpacks.*
- *Catching leaves with our hands as they fell from the trees. Not sure we ever had more fun than that!*
- *You holding Rainey a couple of hours after he was born.*
- *Riding home in the van with baby schnauzer Deacon. Three kids with the biggest smiles I ever saw!*
- *Playing keyboard in the youth worship band at church. You looked so serious.*
- *Coming home after having your wisdom teeth extracted. Earth to Jordan. Earth to Jordan... come in Jordan.*
- *Standing with you, waiting for the bagpiper to lead us down the aisle at your wedding. A moment I had waited for, and dreaded, ever since you were born. Somehow, it was much more wonderful than I ever imagined it would be.*

Looking forward to a hundred more wonderful images of you!

Love,
Dad

Chapter 2 Emotional pain: Fingerprints of the human experience

Everyone who has fingers has fingerprints. It is one of the many things we humans have in common that also make us unique, which is something of a paradox. Long before the TV show CSI, police officers were using fingerprint information to identify and convict criminals. The first time fingerprints were used in a criminal investigation was in 1892 in Buenos Aires when a cop named Juan Vucetich was working on a double-homicide[6]. Two boys had been murdered. A man romantically linked to the mother of the boys was the prime suspect, but when Vucetich compared fingerprints found at the crime scene with those of the man and the boys' mother, he discovered they matched those of the mother exactly. This discovery led to the mother's confession.[7] Sherlock Holmes, who made his first literary appearance just five years earlier, would have been delighted by such fine detective work.

Just as every person has a unique fingerprint, every person has a unique story of personal pain and

36

anguish. My story involves drug addiction, financial loss, business problems and several other woes. Yours may be chronic illness, a destroyed relationship, mental health issues, the tragic death of a loved one or some terrible combination of these. Every person's life experience is unique. Furthermore, from my own observations it seems as though every human being is dealing with a significant problem, either personally or through a relationship. So, life problems are both unique and common to us all. Our problems may vary in severity and complexity, but we all have them. If you have never had a serious life challenge, then you either have not lived long enough or you are uncommonly blessed (and I want to swap lives with you).

   If you are dealing with a serious life challenge, then you also are likely battling the emotional and psychological problems that often accompany a major crisis. This is a natural human reaction. A major life crisis brings with it uncertainty; we don't know what the outcome will be and the possibilities may be frightening to consider. A problem such as the infidelity of a spouse may raise the question, "Will our marriage survive?" or, "Does he/she love me anymore?" Financial problems lead you to worry about bank-ruptcy, losing your home, or worse. The death of a loved one creates enormous uncertainty. You wonder if you will ever stop grieving. You worry about your future without this person in your life. Your stress may involve the loved one's relationship with God and their eternal home. These uncertainties weigh heavily on the mind and contribute greatly to depression and anxiety. Is it any wonder that one in 10 Americans now take antidepressants? Among women ages 40-50 the ratio is one-in-four.[8]

From a human perspective, your problem may seem insurmountable, like the Himalayan mountain Annapurna. At 26,545 feet, Annapurna is "only" the tenth tallest mountain in the world, but may be the most difficult and dangerous to climb. As of 2012, only 191 people have successfully climbed it, and more than 60 have died trying[9]. Even experienced mountaineers consider Annapurna intimidating and frightening. Many give up before they reach the summit; others never try. Facing a gigantic life challenge is like that. It may seem too big and too difficult. It creates fear and anxiety, worry and even depression as you realize that it is a mountain you may never climb.

Sherry Welch faced an Annapurna of problems in 2001 and 2002. In a span of 11 months she endured a maelstrom of misfortunes that would humble even the most faithful Christian.

- Oct., 2001 – Her husband, Doug, is diagnosed with cancer of the esophagus.
- February 2002 – Her dad is diagnosed with a malignant facial tumor.

- March 2002 – She discovers she has breast cancer.
- March 2002 – Her oldest son admits heroin addiction and attempts suicide.
- July 31, 2002 – Doug dies.
- August 31, 2002 – Her father dies.

Any one of those problems would create enormous emotional stress. Sherry Welch endured all of them in less than a year. Sherry, who lives in Baltimore, is my sister-in-law and I saw her at her father's funeral in '02, about four weeks after her husband's death. Her hair had not fully grown in from her chemotherapy treatments and she was still mourning Doug, yet she summoned the courage to speak at her father's graveside service and even led the attendees in singing along with a recorded version of Elvis Presley's "How Great Thou Art." Like the other women in her family, she's pretty tough.

"I had a lot of anxiety at that time; anxiety about my ability to deal with all of the problems at the same time. I had a lot of anxiety about Kathryn (her daughter), who was only in the eighth grade then, and there was a lot of anxiety about my son's addiction." Sherry answered the questions without having to ponder them. She has had 12 years to contemplate the mountain she overcame, so the answers come easier now, with fewer tears. "I believe you go to God and lay it all out and He will respond, but we may not

39

understand or agree with His response. God's response to my prayers was peace and clarity, not healing for Doug. He gave me peace when it became evident that there was nothing more we could do about Doug's cancer, and He gave me the clarity and strength to help my three kids get through it all. Were there tears? Oh yeah. I still have moments of grief and sadness, but the moments of peace are much greater and deeper. It's this overarching sense of peace that I define as the 'peace that surpasses all understanding.' We still miss Doug, but God has restored our family. He promises us peace, not perfection."

No, life is not perfect, not by a long shot, and Sherry's peace may not be perfect, but it is sufficient to sustain her. And, believe it or not, she is happy for the experience.

"I'm grateful we went through all of it because it helped me to overcome so much fear." She said this smiling, with complete sincerity. "I'm no longer afraid of dying. I went from arrogance in my own faith to a confidence in God. And He removed the anxiety I had about being both mother and dad to my children. I'm just so joyful for the peace we have as a family now."

The 11th chapter of Luke contains an exchange between Jesus and the disciples that provides a great example of God's paternal instincts toward us. This is the chapter in which Jesus provides His example of the model prayer, which we know as the Lord's Prayer. In

40

the verses that follow Jesus's prayer, He explains God's goodness by stating,

"What father among you, if his son asks for a fish, will instead of a fish give him a serpent; or if he asks for an egg, will give him a scorpion? If you then, who are evil, know how to give good gifts to your children, how much more will the heavenly Father give the Holy Spirit to those who ask him!" (Luke 11:11-13)

Believers who are begging God regarding an urgent need often use this verse to "remind" God that, as a loving Father, He should give us what we ask for. I did this when we were praying for our daughter's recovery and for my business when it was in danger of collapsing. Certainly, God is a loving Father who wants to give His children good gifts, but He is also GOD, and His ways are higher than our ways (Isaiah 55:9). We cannot possibly know His entire plan for our lives or for His Kingdom, and He may allow things to happen that we simply can't understand. Sometimes it is something for our own good, the good of someone else, or a greater good that we can't know about with our limited perspective on humanity and eternity. The situation is a little like a small child who is perplexed when their parents allow a nurse to administer a painful injection. Why would mommy let this person hurt me? What the child doesn't understand is the greater good that comes from that pain – protection against a serious virus and the further spread of that

41

virus. Often God's plan involves a greater good, something we cannot understand in the moment. That moment, and the time that follows it, can be very painful, but for the believer the pain has a purpose even if we cannot see it in the moment.

In 2009, Whitney and B.J. Clay were expecting their first baby, a girl they named Callie. The baby was something of a celebrity in their church even before she was born because Whitney is a youth pastor and dozens of her students had watched her progression through the pregnancy with great anticipation. Callie would no doubt be smothered with attention from many loving "big sisters" who were more than ready to be baby sitters. Likewise, many adults in the church eagerly anticipated Callie's birth because Whitney and B.J. were so beloved and involved in the life of the church. In a sense, Callie would be everyone's new baby.

Callie's problem was first detected at a routine ultrasound procedure. Initially the doctors suspected some internal malformations and perhaps even Down Syndrome, but subsequent testing revealed the specific problem to be in Callie's intestines; they were twisted and would require surgery immediately after delivery. The surgeon assured them that the procedure was relatively routine and that she would likely be just fine. They monitored her development carefully over the remaining weeks of Whitney's pregnancy and when Callie was born after 40 weeks, she was a very robust 9 pounds, 5 ounces. Whitney, who delivered the baby via caesarian section, had a brief moment to touch her baby's hand and face before Callie and B.J. were taken, as planned, by ambulance to a nearby hospital that specializes in neonatal surgery. What the doctors discovered when they began their work was more serious than they had anticipated; Callie's gall bladder was missing, her appendix was much smaller than normal, her spleen was on the wrong side of her body and her intestines were twisted in two places. In the autopsy they would discover her lungs were also very underdeveloped for a full-term baby. She survived the surgery, but not for long. Callie's life lasted merely 15 hours. A few days later Whitney held her baby for the first time, just minutes before the funeral.

"I felt that God abandoned us," said B.J., who teaches a Sunday School class, plays guitar in the church worship band and has mentored dozens of young boys in their faith. "I told God, 'I do all this stuff to serve You and this is what I get? It isn't right.' Later I blamed myself and asked God what I had done to deserve this type of punishment."

"The first year after her death, everything was hard," Whitney admitted. "I spent hours reading the story of Job and asking God, 'what happened?' We tried to get pregnant again right away, but God didn't allow it. I know now that we weren't ready. I struggled spiritually, wondering how a good God would deny us the gift of healing Callie. A good friend and my former youth pastor, Tom Waring, explained it to me. He said, 'God did not take Callie's life; Callie's death was the result of a fallen, sinful world. The world we live in is not what God intended. He created a perfect place for us, but man rebelled against Him. God grieves over Callie's death. He is a good God who wants good things for us, but we will not live in a perfect world until Jesus returns. Until then there will be pain, death and sorrow. It is our enemy, Satan, who wants to kill and destroy.' Tom's explanation put things into perspective for me. God is a good Father who loves us and we will understand His complete love, and His plan for us, when we are with Him in heaven."

God's mercy and timing are perfect, even if we don't realize it at the time. Nearly two years later Whitney and B.J. were back in the same hospital and same delivery room to welcome a healthy son, Caleb Danger Clay. Yep, his middle name is Danger. He looked very much like his sister at birth, though smaller. Today he is a beautiful and sweet toddler who is being raised in the Ephesians 6:4 way: "Fathers, do not provoke your children to anger, but bring them up in the discipline and instruction of the Lord." Recently they had another child, Carleigh. She, too, seems healthy and perfect.

Sitting across a restaurant table from this wonderful couple, I asked them how they view Callie's life and death now. "Overall, it was a positive experience," said Whitney. She smiled slightly and shared a glance with her husband that others could never understand. "I learned to love people more, to be more compassionate and relate better to those who are hurting. I also think it has made us better parents. I would never want to go through it again, but it has made us better people. What Satan meant for evil…"

Whitney stopped without finishing her sentence. She was paraphrasing the well-known passage from Genesis 50 where Joseph explains to his brothers, the same brothers who sold him into slavery, that God had taken a terrible situation and used it to help and restore them. Whitney and B.J. will always carry around a bit of pain when they think of the beautiful child who was part of their family for 15 hours, but now they look forward to an eternity with her in heaven. "It makes heaven more real to me," explained B.J. "And our faith in God is stronger."

I asked Whitney and B.J. if they believed in the unsurpassed peace that is offered in Philippians 4:7. "God's peace is a type of peace that is hard to understand, at least initially," Whitney explained. "I don't understand everything that happened or why it had to happen, but I learned that I have to trust God,

45

even if I don't understand how or why, and that gives me great peace. You just have to trust God. His peace will protect you."

Inevitably, everyone who goes through a crisis asks the question, "why me?" Maybe the more realistic question is, "why not me?" Sadness and pain come into the life of every human being. No one is immune or exempt from suffering. But, those who are followers of Jesus have a promise, the promise that our Father will help us as we deal with the grief and that He will redeem the situation in His timing. His redemption may come during our mortal life or in our life with Him in Heaven, but it will come. Be confident that God is a loving Father that gives good gifts to His children, so long as we seek His glory and honor above all.

September 1, 2011

Dear Lefty,

> *"Pray the largest prayers. You cannot think a prayer so large that God, in answering it, will not wish you had made it larger. Pray not for crutches but for wings!"*
>
> *Phillips Brooks*

I came across this quote about 15 years ago as I was writing a prayer handbook for our church. Of all the thousands of things I have written in my lifetime, I never wrote anything that had more of an impact on me. A lot of research went into that little handbook, and I learned a lot about what prayer is and what it is not. We assume that prayer is an opportunity to share what is on our heart with God. But doesn't an omniscient God already know what's on our heart? What, then, is the purpose of prayer?

Worship and faith.

We were created to <u>worship</u> God. That's a fundamental fact that few people ever learn. Those who don't worship God are worshipping something else. We all worship something – money, self, other gods... Everyone is going to worship something, and *if you aren't worshipping Jehovah God, your life is going to get out of synch.*

You can learn a lot about <u>faith</u> by reading Hebrews 11, but it doesn't explain faith in a way that is perfectly clear for a dolt like me. I've thought long and hard about the subject and have come to some simple conclusions. Faith is simply knowing that God is. He is real – as real as you or I. He is the creator, the Alpha and Omega, timeless, omnipotent... all that stuff and more. He is far greater than we can imagine with our puny human brains. He loves me and will do what's best for me. He is capable of anything. He wants us to test His love and greatness. He wants to bless us so we can be a blessing to others.

I want to pray bigger prayers. I want to totally submit to God. I want to have gigantic faith and KNOW that God is going to do something miraculous. Let's dream about what God could do with our lives if we give them to Him. The next few years could be incredible for all of us if we have the faith to BELIEVE.

I hope God gives you an extraordinary and unique blessing today – something totally unexpected and cool.

Love,
Dad

Chapter 3 Spiritual warfare: Your heart, mind and soul are the battleground

"For we do not wrestle against flesh and blood, but against the rulers, against the authorities, against the cosmic powers over this present darkness, against the spiritual forces of evil in the heavenly places." Ephesians 6:12

I "accepted the Lord" when I was seven years old, though I didn't fully understand what that meant at the time. What I was really looking for was fire insurance. I came under conviction at a drive-in movie, sitting in the back seat of my brother-in-law's car. The movie playing that night was "Back Door To Hell," a war picture that was only notable because one of its stars was a very young Jack Nicholson. I had no interest in the movie, but the title got me thinking about something our pastor had said recently regarding God's judgment. You either go to heaven or hell, depending on where you stand with Jesus. I had become aware that I was a sinner. The very next week I spoke with our pastor privately and he explained everything. He led me in the sinner's prayer and I joined God's family. A few weeks later I was baptized.

I grew up attending church (thanks, Mother), but like many who become believers at an early age, my relationship with the Lord waxed and waned. I went off to college with the idea that I would experience real life. I wanted to prove I was not some hick from a small town, so I looked for the cool crowd and sleazed my way into their company. It was the late-70s and sex, drugs and rock-and-roll were the benchmarks of college life. I fully embraced them.

God is often merciful to fools, and He was merciful to me even in the years of my rebellion. In His goodness he allowed me to find my soul mate, Tracy Phifer. Like me, she had grown up attending church and was a nominal Christian, but she really had no concept of "born again" belief or a real relationship with Jesus. Over time we found a great church and began to learn what it meant to be disciples of Jesus Christ. We are still learning, but I can say that we both genuinely love God and want to serve Him. Our faith and future in eternity are secure.

When I became a Christian at seven, and later as my faith began to mature in my 20s and 30s, I did not realize that I had been enlisted in an army that was fighting a spiritual war. Hey, I was only in this for the fire insurance, remember? Instead, I was now a soldier and an enemy of the devil in the battle between good and evil. As my relationship with Jesus grew, so did the intensity of the spiritual attacks by Satan. I began to fully understand the implications of Ephesians 6:12. Fortunately, I had good Bible teachers over the years who taught me the rest of that chapter. If you read on in Ephesians 6, it encourages us to "put on the full armor of God." When our big troubles began in 2011, my wife and I hunkered down behind the shield of faith to withstand the "flaming arrows" of the enemy. That's a very useful verse in times of tribulation, but that verse alone will not save you from fear and anxiety.

Being a sold-out, committed follower of Jesus does not mean your faith is always like Gibraltar. In fact, it is your faith in Jesus that makes Satan so angry, and he will do everything in his power to destroy it and ruin your life. He knows that a single attack may not buckle your belief, but a relentless assault over a long period of time might cause you to give up. Consider the story of Job. Few books in the Bible contain as much practical theology as the account of Job. In case you are unfamiliar with Job, he was an extremely wealthy and successful man who lived at least 2000 years before Christ. He had a wife and 10 children. You could say he was living the American dream, except he lived in a place called Uz, which was likely somewhere east of the Sea of Galilee. He also was a very good man who is described as "blameless and upright, one who feared God and turned away from evil" (Job 1:1). To borrow a line from the movie *Ferris Bueller's Day Off*, he was a righteous dude. His goodness and devotion to God infuriated Satan, who attributed Job's righteousness to God's favor over him. One day, the Bible says, Satan had a conversation with God. To paraphrase, the devil said, "sure Job loves you, but it is because you've given him everything a man could want. I'll bet if you take away all his money and blessings, he'll curse you to your face." The Lord, who knows every heart, told Satan he could test Job. "Do anything you want," said God, "you just can't touch him." Satan unleashed an incredible attack, killing all of Job's livestock, which was his source of wealth, and then killing all of his children as well. Job, though grief stricken, remained faithful. Satan then went back to God and asked for permission to attack Job himself. God acquiesced, and Job became covered head to toe in painful boils. Think about all of your problems for a moment. Are they as bad as those faced by Job? Probably not. Nevertheless, your problems are still significant and perhaps even life-threatening. To you, they are a matter of life and death. And like Job, you may not understand why they have occurred.

There is a long account in the book of Job about a conversation Job had with a group of three friends. Basically, they speculate that Job must have committed some terrible sin for which he was being punished. Job's wife even recommended that he "curse God and die." But Job staunchly defended his behavior and he correctly understood a very critical point of faith: God is sovereign, which is a churchy word that means He has control over everything. God eventually restored Job's wealth to even greater levels and gave him 10 more children, making him the Jim Bob Duggar of the ancient world. The story also mentions that in all the land there were no women as lovely as Job's daughters. Perhaps one of them became "Miss Uz," though I doubt they had a swimsuit competition.

In chapter 13 Job makes an interesting statement about the great value of a relationship with God. In verse 16 of that chapter he states, "This will be my salvation, that the godless shall not come before him." Job knew that the godless will have no audience before God. He was confident, however, in *his* relationship with the Lord and knew he would have an opportunity to face God personally and have a chance to plead his case before the Father. Job is saying what every Christian must come to understand: A personal relationship with the Lord is the most valuable thing a person can possess, but it does not exempt you from pain and suffering (or anxiety and fear). God often allows bad circumstances to happen in life. Maybe the problems have occurred to help refine and grow your faith, or maybe they are simply an act of "life happening." God did not cause your wife to leave you after 20 years of marriage; she may have left because sin overwhelmed her good judgment and caused her to forget her vows. Stuff happens, to paraphrase Forrest Gump, largely because we live in a world of fallen, sinful people. Their sins affect others, and your sins affect them. These events do not surprise God because he is omnipotent, another churchy word that means He has supreme power and authority over everything. The problems in your life may grieve Him, but He allows them to happen, often for your own spiritual good or sometimes simply as a result of your, or someone else's, bad decisions. The devil will try to use these situations to crush your happiness and damage your relationship with God. Meanwhile, our Holy Father urges us to remain faithful and wait for His appearing. Consider Paul's message to Timothy:

"I have fought the good fight, I have finished the race, I have kept the faith. Henceforth there is laid up for me the crown of righteousness, which the Lord, the righteous judge, will award to me on that Day, and not only to me but also to all who have loved his appearing." - 2 Timothy 4:7-8

Life is happening all the time, and some of it is very unpleasant. God is telling us, Keep Calm and Carry On.

54

As Sherry Welch explained, "life is a battle between chaos and reasonableness. Chaotic things happen in life. Is it reasonable to expect a happy life all the time? I don't think so. You must be willing to accept the fact that bad things may happen that we can't fully understand."

"When you dig a well, you might fall in. When you demolish an old wall, you could be bitten by a snake. When you work in a quarry, stones might fall and crush you. When you chop wood, there is danger with each stroke of your ax! Such are the risks of life." (Ecclesiastes 10:8-9)

Job understood that bad things happen to good people. But just knowing that does not make anxiety or fear go away. He was suffering, sad and resentful. His only option was to plead his case before God. He also knew – and this is important – that those who do not have a relationship with God do not have access to the Creator of the universe and the lover of their soul. Some 2,000 years later Jesus would clarify things by stating, *"I am the way, the truth and the life. No one comes to the Father except through me"* (John 14:6). We must commit our lives to Jesus to have access to God, and God is our only hope for peace when the world is collapsing on us.

At first I did not consider the possibility that the problems we were having in 2011-2013 were attacks from Satan. Spiritual warfare was, to me, something of an abstract concept. Spiritual warfare was an ethereal, intangible battle between good and evil that goes on every day. I thought it was all about making the right or wrong choices, like when you choose to eat a cheeseburger and fries rather than a spinach salad. American advertising loves to portray the little devil on one shoulder and the angel on the other. "Go ahead, you know you want it!" "Stop! Remember your cholesterol." It's all so cute. In real life, Satan and his demons are trying to ruin your life. Their goal is to destroy your family, wreck you financially, lead you into various addictions, distract you from the gospel and make you doubt that God even exists. The devil has no pity and will use anything he can to take you down, even if it means attacking your children. It is deadly serious business, yet we 21st Century Christians constantly flirt with sin and invite the devil to gain a foothold. We drift around on the Internet, glancing at provocative content. Oh, one of the Kardashians has released another sex tape. Wonder what that's about? Once we've become desensitized, we move on to soft porn and eventually XXX-rated sites. We use Facebook and Twitter to exchange gossip or fuel controversy. We watch R-rated movies and sex-saturated sitcoms, allowing that content to pollute our thoughts and conversation. Our churches twist or simply ignore clear Biblical principles to fit current cultural mores, just to avoid conflict and "remain relevant" in modern society. Satan is always trying to subvert believers. It's what he does and he is working at it constantly. He is an expert saboteur, a bomb-throwing terrorist who wants to hurt people. The bottom line: spiritual warfare is real and we often open the gates and allow the enemy inside.

My own personal spiritual warfare was an attack on multiple fronts. Satan's battle plan began with an exploitation of a weakness in my defenses. I had become complacent and overconfident in my own spiritual life. My wife and I have spent a lot of time in retrospection over the past three years, and as I look back, I can see how pride had crept in and weakened my defenses. In 2010 I could survey my life and be pleased. I had a happy family, healthy and smart kids, a great job, a high position in church, a nice house that was paid for and plenty of good friends. In retrospect, I was a little like the parable in Luke 12; "*soul, you have ample goods laid up for many years; relax, eat, drink and be merry.*" Satan had a foothold; I was fat, dumb and happy. My idols were my family, my stature in the church and my career. I was an easy target.

It is interesting to note that God *wants* us to focus much attention on our families, to work hard and be successful, and to be leaders in church if we are appropriately gifted (*"The saying is trustworthy: If anyone aspires to the office of overseer, he desires a noble task."* 1 Timothy 3:1). However, if these things get out of order on your priority list, they become idols. Even though I projected the image of a humble servant of God – just about anyone who knows me would say that I'm a relatively humble guy – the fact was, I was pretty pleased with myself. I had succeeded in every area of life, or so I thought. I idolized my family, my career and my status at church. In 2010 I thought I was fully engaged in God's army and fighting the devil. I didn't realize that, up until then, I had only experienced skirmishes and the real battle was about to begin.

My older sister Deborah is a mature Christ-follower. She and her husband, Freddie, have experienced some really tough times: Freddie became deaf in his thirties, they went bankrupt and lost their family business, they've seen their children go through significant personal struggles... typical life tragedies. She was among the first to correctly identify our situation when we described all the issues that had beset us. "This is spiritual warfare." She said it with the confidence of an experienced physician diagnosing the flu. "You are being attacked by Satan." I had been very reluctant to consider our troubles as spiritual warfare because, in my own thinking, "Why would the devil even worry about singling us out for attack? Shouldn't he be more concerned with pastors and missionaries and Billy Graham? Those folks are way bigger threats than me." That was spiritual naivety on my part. Satan is an equal-opportunity tormentor. He wants to derail every believer. Given an opportunity, he will strike. In our case, he saw a prideful man with idols in his life. Even worse, I was oblivious to my own spiritual weaknesses. Like America before Pearl Harbor, I thought I was protected and mostly immune to attack. The bombs in my life shattered my peace and wounded my heart (family), my soul (faith) and my mind (sanity).

The devil attacks Christians in order to destroy their relationship with God, but we must remember that he cannot take us away from our Heavenly Father.

"I give them eternal life, and they will never perish, and no one will snatch them out of my hand. My Father, who has given them to me, is greater than all, and no one is able to snatch them out of the Father's hand. I and the Father are one." John 10:28-30

Though we are safe in our Father's hand, Satan knows that if our lives are shattered we may become distracted, doubt our salvation and become ineffective as disciples. Satan wants our eyes focused on our problems, not on the One who can solve them. In warfare, they call this a diversionary tactic. That was certainly true in my case. For months I was totally consumed with my daughter's health and my business problems. I also was very worried about how Jordan's addiction was affecting our two younger children and our son-in-law, who was staying with us much of the time. I was wracked with self-doubt – how did we fail as parents? Why didn't I see this coming? I became very fearful about everything. I worried constantly about the future and the "what ifs." What if she relapses? What if she runs away? What if she over-doses? What if her husband gives up on her? What if one of my other kids falls into addiction? What if my business fails? I had worry for breakfast, stress for lunch and despair for dinner. And even when a ray of sunshine would appear, other dark clouds would immediately move in – more business worries, my son's disappointments in baseball, the usual life problems... I prayed for relief from worry and stress, but relief came only by moments; I usually slid quickly back into anxiety. This made me very concerned that my relationship with the Lord was somehow flawed. Was I such a weak Christian that I could not maintain my faith? Was I even "saved" at all? At church we put on our brave faces and shared that "we can see God's hand at work." Privately, I wasn't so sure. Plus, I wondered how long I could hold out. I worried that, at some point, the problems would become so overwhelming that I would give up and curse God. I was not Job. Maybe I would go crazy from the stress and have a nervous breakdown. Maybe I should start using drugs myself. A joint might help me relax. I wondered where I could get one.

This is how madness can overtake a believer. This is how Satan wins the spiritual war.

September 2, 2011

Dear Lefty,

As you know, Christmas has always been special in the Gibbs household. We truly embrace Christmas, and maybe not always for the right reasons. I'm sure you would agree that some of our best memories were made at Christmastime. When you guys were little bitty, we used to make a big deal about writing letters to Santa. Here is one from the early days. Love the way you sucked up to Santa by mentioning Mrs. Claus, and note the request for a "Spider-graph" and "puppy surprise!" Also, it was so nice of you to throw a request in there for Haley, who was 1 at the time. Maybe reading this will help you get into the spirit extra early this year!

Love,
Dad

December 7, 1992

Mr. Santa Claus
North Pole

Dear Santa:

Hello. How are you? I hope you have had a nice year. Thank you for my presents last Christmas. I really liked my new Barbie bicycle very much. I hope Mrs. Santa is feeling well. Please tell her hello for me.

I have been an extra good girl this year. Please bring me some new toys. Here are some of the things I would like. A Beauty & the Beast Barbie doll and clothes, a Spider-graph, a Barbie house, new Christmas clothes for me, a new game to play, and a puppy surprise. If you could bring me these things, I really would appreciate it.

Also, I have a little sister named Haley. Please bring her some nice new toys like a rattle, a wagon, and a baby doll.

Thank you Santa for being so nice. Be careful delivering the toys on Christmas Eve.

Your friend,
Jordan Gibbs

Chapter 4 The importance of Scripture

"When you read God's Word, you must constantly be saying to yourself, "It is talking to me, and about me." Soren Kierkegaard

We had something of a tradition on our high school football team whereby seniors were allowed, maybe even encouraged, to pick on the first-year players. Typically, a senior player would select one of the new guys as a special target to persecute. The coaches tacitly promoted this behavior by sometimes allowing the seniors to select a younger guy to go against in one-on-one drills. My tormentor was a senior all-conference lineman named Matt. At least once or twice a week Matt would select me from the lineup of greenhorns to be his tackling dummy in one of the numerous collision drills the coaches devised. I'd line up against Matt snarling and coiled up, ready to strike, only to be flattened by my older, stronger, larger and much tougher opponent. This became our routine as the season wore on. One day, before practice, I found myself sitting on a sideline bench waiting for our workout to begin. I was in full pads with my helmet on, unstrapped. I noticed from the corner of my eye, Matt, strolling along the sideline, nonchalantly. As he came in front of me, he reached down with his big right paw and grabbed my face mask, pulling me to my feet. With great force he jerked my head forward in order to bang our helmets together. This was something football players sometimes do either to fire themselves up and prepare for the upcoming battle, or to intimidate younger and smaller guys, which was the case in this instance. Our heads cracked together, but I was unharmed. Matt, who had far more brawn than brains, staggered backwards, suffering from a self-inflicted near concussion. You see, he forgot to put on his own helmet; it was in his other hand. As for me, you could say I was wearing the helmet of salvation.

In Ephesians, Paul gives us vital information about spiritual warfare and how we can not only defend ourselves, but also fight back. He informs us that our enemy is not made of flesh and blood, but is a "mighty power of darkness." If we attempt to battle this foe without the proper armor, we are certainly going to get hurt. Paul encourages us to use "every piece" of the armor God provides: the belt of truth, the breastplate of righteousness, the shoes of peace (the gospel or good news of Jesus), the shield of faith, the helmet of salvation and the sword of the Word of God. With such protection, how can the devil harm us!

What I learned in my spiritual battle experience is that even if you are wearing the armor, you often can feel the weight of the blows as they strike you. Furthermore, Satan will keep swinging his hammer until you are weary. He is relentless, always looking for a weakness, an opening so that he can do harm emotionally, spiritually or psychologically (heart, soul, mind). Spiritual warfare is exhausting and it is not uncommon for a believer to let down their guard. That's why it is essential to stay close to God, especially when under attack. We can do this by praying constantly, reading the Word consistently and trying always to maintain an attitude of worship. This tripod of prayer, Scripture and worship will keep you upright and on balance when Satan slams you. Doing any one of these is good, doing two is better, but it takes all three to maintain steadiness in a spiritual attack. It is simply impossible to overstate the importance of Scripture reading, worship and prayer as you endure difficult ordeals.

"For the word of God is living and active, sharper than any two-edged sword, piercing to the division of soul and of spirit, of joints and of marrow, and discerning the thoughts and intentions of the heart." Hebrews 4:12

I've read the Bible from front to back. A few years ago I began in Genesis and read completely through Revelations. Over my lifetime I've read and reread many of the most important passages multiple times. The specific book of the Bible I am reading at any given time depends on what's going on in my life. Psalms is great for both comfort and praising God. The Gospels are good to read when you want to know Jesus better. The New Testament Epistles provide lots of practical advice for believers. I try to read the Word every day, if only for a few minutes. It's important because the Bible is one of the ways in which God communicates with us and encourages us in difficult circumstances.

On a few wonderful and rare occasions, God has spoken to me directly from His Word. In one situation, it literally changed my life. In 1992 I was struggling in my job as a young advertising account executive. Through what I would describe as a miraculous revealing of His will through Scripture, I quit my job at a successful Memphis ad agency and began a freelance career. I did this based solely on a few verses of Scripture God gave me at a crucial moment. I had been struggling with the question, "God, is this you telling me to quit my job, or is it the evil one, wanting me to ruin my career by quitting the best job I ever had?" One morning at work, immediately after praying those exact words, I looked down at a Bible lying open on my desk. It was Matthew, chapter 14, the story of Jesus walking on the water. I read, "'Lord, if it's really you, tell me to come to you by walking on the water.' 'All right, come,' Jesus said." I swallowed hard. In my heart, Jesus had just spoken directly to me and said, "Get out of the boat!" That afternoon I gave my two-weeks notice. Following God's advice as I found it in Scripture was the best career move I ever made. He not only blessed me professionally and financially, but He gave me more free time to devote to Christian causes, including an unpaid second job working for a church-planting organization called Eagle Projects International. Fast-forward more than 23 years and I now serve on the Eagle Projects Board of Directors.

My experience in 1992 changed my attitude about reading the Bible. I now saw that the Word of God was not just a lot of good advice or historical information about God, it was often a direct line of communication from our Heavenly Father to me. I discovered that God could speak to me – and answer my questions – directly through His Word. I should note that God does not always choose to answer your questions directly with a verse of Scripture at just the right time, as He did for me in 1992. At other times He has revealed His answers in more subtle ways – through the advice of a trusted friend, or through a gradual process of spiritual revelation. But the Bible is perhaps the most direct method for obtaining God's

68

advice and should be the first place we go in times of distress.

The news of our daughter's addiction was a thunderbolt. We were scared and anxious, uncertain of what might happen next. My wife adopted a verse in those early days as a rallying cry. It's found in 2 Corinthians:

"We are afflicted in every way, but not crushed; perplexed, but not driven to despair; persecuted, but not forsaken; struck down, but not destroyed." 2 Corinthians 4:8-9

This was the first of many verses God gave us during our struggles in 2011-13. Christians often view Bible reading as a task that must be accomplished every day, like sit-ups or taking a multivitamin. If you want to be spiritually healthy, get yourself a good dose of the Good Book. While it is helpful to read the Word each day, even if just for the sake of being obedient, you probably don't get the full benefit unless you read the Bible with a purpose. When believers face life-challenging circumstances, the Bible should be considered an essential part of your life. It is the tourniquet in your crisis survival kit, helping to prevent the excessive loss of sanity. God uses His Word to provide wisdom for your situation, context for your problem and hope for the future. His words are the arm around your shoulder that keeps you upright when you are ready to collapse, and He seems to

69

know exactly what you need to hear at the moment you need to hear it. During our tribulation I often felt like someone who had fallen into a rushing mountain stream; I was being carried away by the current, frightened and about to drown. These passages from the Lord were to me like rocks on which to cling. At just the right time He would provide a verse that seemed to speak to my situation that day. I would hang on to that verse and re-read it every time I felt anxiety start to overtake me. I compiled a list of life-saving verses over those many long months. These were the words the Holy Spirit was whispering in my ear, keeping me moving forward when I was spiritually paralyzed. It was a private communion with God that I would not have had if my life had remained happy and uncomplicated. The Lord was using my personal turmoil to pull me closer to Him.

10 passages that can be a life preserver when you are sinking in despair:

"Do not be anxious about anything, but in everything by prayer and supplication with thanksgiving let your requests be made known to God." Philippians 4:6

"Fear not, for I am with you; be not dismayed, for I am your God; I will strengthen you, I will help

you, I will uphold you with my righteous right hand." Isaiah 41:10

"I have said these things to you, that in me you may have peace. In the world you will have tribulation. But take heart; I have overcome the world." John 16:33

"God is our refuge and strength, a very present help in trouble. Therefore, we will not fear though the earth gives way, though the mountains be moved into the heart of the sea, though its waters roar and foam, though the mountains tremble at its swelling." Psalms 46:1-3

"Let not your hearts be troubled. Believe in God; believe also in me." John 14:1

"May the God of hope fill you with all joy and peace as you trust in Him, so that you may overflow with hope by the power of the Holy Spirit." Romans 15:13

"The Lord is a stronghold for the oppressed, a stronghold in times of trouble. And those who know your name put their trust in you, for you, O LORD, have not forsaken those who seek you." Psalms 9:9-10

"So we do not lose heart. Though our outer self is wasting away, our inner self is being renewed day by day. For this light momentary affliction is preparing for us an eternal weight of glory beyond all comparison, as we look not to the things that are seen but to the things that are unseen. For the things that are seen are transient, but the things that are unseen are eternal." 2 Corinthians 4:16-18

"Therefore I tell you, do not be anxious about your life, what you will eat or what you will drink, nor about your body, what you will put on. Is not life more than food, and the body more than clothing? Look at the birds of the air: they neither sow nor reap nor gather into barns, and yet your heavenly Father feeds them. Are you not of more value than they?" Matthew 6:25-26

"Likewise the Spirit helps us in our weakness. For we do not know what to pray for as we ought, but the Spirit himself intercedes for us with groanings too deep for words. And he who searches hearts knows what is the mind of the Spirit, because the Spirit intercedes for the saints according to the will of God. And we know that for those who love God all things work together for good, for those who are called according to his purpose." Romans 8:26-28

That last passage in Romans, chapter 8, is well known by many believers. It was the passage cited often by my older brother, "Buzzy" Gibbs when he would call me to provide encouragement. That is his favorite verse in the Bible, the cornerstone on which he builds his daily faith. It is a verse every believer should know in a season of crisis, because it may be your own personal life preserver during the storm. It would be a prophetic verse for me as the next two years unfolded.

September 3, 2011

Dear Lefty,

The Germantown Station Park at the end of our cove is one of my favorite places in the whole world, and it's only 50 steps from our front door. How convenient! I love the park because on most days I have it all to myself. I can take Deacon for a walk and think about something other than work. For 30 minutes a day – two dog walks – I can relax.

Sometimes, when I am particularly troubled about some issue in my life, I sit down on one of the benches and pray. I've had some serious talks with God sitting by that pond. I also spend a lot of time looking for fish. We have a number of small bass right now and by next spring, they should be big enough to catch.

How many great memories do we have at the park? About a thousand, at least. I played catch there with each one of you kids, and taught each of you to hit a ball. We have played Frisbee golf, horseshoes, hide-and-go-seek and tag. We've flown kites and launched rockets. We've had picnics and played on the playground. Remember the old playground? It was made of wood. Either you or Haley got splinters in your butt; can't remember which of you that was. I felt terrible for you at the time, but it seems funny in retrospect.

My very favorite memories of the park are the Easter egg hunts. Seeing my little angels dash around with a hundred other kids, looking for eggs that were hidden in plain site, how wonderful is that for a parent? It's too bad you girls were so afraid of the dude in the Easter bunny costume. I would have loved to have some photos, but you and Haley ran away in terror any time the EB showed up.

The park is awesome when we have a big snowfall or deep freeze. I love the look of snow on the evergreen trees. I'll never forget walking to the park during a long period of very cold weather. The ice on the pond was about four inches thick. Some kids had taken one of those big, heavy picnic tables and pushed it out onto the ice. I had to give them an A+ for creative mischief.

Normally at this time of year the park is mostly brown as the heat and dry weather have scorched the grass, but we've had a lot of rain over the past two months and everything is still beautiful and green.

It's almost time to take Deacon for another walk. When you get home, we'll walk the park together. I can't wait!

Love,
Dad

Chapter 5 The value of worship

For the record, worship is not just singing. We often refer to "worship" as that period of time in church before preaching when the talented, musical people lead the tone deaf in songs of praise. Singing may be a form of worship, but it is not the *only* way to worship. Worship is any way that we can raise our affections toward God. Maybe your worship is through acts of service (my wife loves to cook for people) or through teaching a Sunday School class. Maybe you worship as you read the Bible. Our pastor likes to remind our congregation that tithing – giving 10 percent of our income to the local church – is an act of worship, and I agree. I've heard some people say they worship when they go fishing or play golf, usually on Sunday. I don't want to doubt their sincerity, but actually, I do. You can theoretically worship doing anything, but actual worship usually involves a measure of reverence, time and sacrifice. I've been told the etymology of the word involves the phrase "worth-ship," as if you are attributing great worth to something through reverence, time and sacrifice. That makes sense to me. Some people worship money, some worship football, and a lot of people worship themselves. You can usually tell what a person worships by the amount of time they spend talking about it. People who talk about themselves or their interests all the time usually worship at the church of "ME." I have to check myself regularly to make sure I'm not a member of that church.

Personally, I prefer to worship through prayer. That's largely due to the fact that I am not a singer. My lack of musical gifting can be verified by anyone who has heard me sing. My children often mock and ridicule me when I sing around the house, and my wife simply gives me a look that demands, "Stop doing that *now*." Such negative feedback has led me to the point where I no longer sing in the presence of anyone – all my singing is done in the privacy of my vehicle or when I am alone at home. It makes my two schnauzers howl, but I don't care. The only song I've ever been *requested* to sing is my special rendition of Dolly Parton's "Jolene." My falsetto on the words "Jolene, Jo-lene, JO-LE-EE-ENE," cracks up the kids, though I don't know why.

Nevertheless, despite my complete lack of singing talent, I have come to appreciate praise music. It is both therapeutic in tough times and joyful in times of celebration. Fortunately, we live in an era of wonderful new praise music. Artists such as Chris Tomlin, Michael W. Smith and Lecrae are writing and performing some incredible music. This is not to say that the old hymns are not powerful and inspirational, they are. I'm happy to be old enough to have sung and memorized many classic hymns of faith. I grew up attending a small, rural Baptist church. Our church choir was enthusiastic though mostly devoid of any actual vocal talent. I vividly recall off-key versions of many old standards such as "Leaning On The Everlasting Arms," "It Is Well With My Soul," "All Hail The Power of Jesus Name," and many others. The hymn "In the Garden" has special significance to me because it has been sung at almost every family funeral I have ever attended. I have no idea why this song is so meaningful to my family, but it shows up at every funeral, like an uncle who lives far away. I have only one stipulation for my own funerary arrangements; someone has to sing "In The Garden." The remainder of the event can be a square dance for all I care – I'll be singing "Jolene" with my perfect new voice in paradise.

As I struggled through the events of 2011-2013, I often found myself humming or singing the old hymns I had heard in my youth. The words seemed to pop into my head at just the right moment to help cancel out a worry or fear. I can't explain why these songs came to mind, other than the distinct possibility that the Holy Spirit pulled them from the deepest

recesses of my brain because I needed the encouragement. It was on such a day when I was agonizing over
some new crisis that the words "it is well with my soul"
drifted in like a pleasant aroma coming through the
window.

When peace, like a river, attendeth my way,
When sorrows like sea billows roll;
Whatever my lot, Thou has taught me to say,
It is well, it is well, with my soul.

I had never really thought about those
wonderful lyrics before, but now they had incredible
new meaning and provided great comfort to me. I
even took the time to look up the story of the man
who wrote "It Is Well With My Soul," Horatio Gates
Spafford. Spafford was a prominent Chicago attorney
and wealthy businessman who was a close friend of
the evangelist Dwight Moody. Spafford lost much of
his fortune in the Great Chicago Fire of 1871. Adding
to his misfortune, he later lost all four of his daughters
in a shipwreck. Later, while crossing the Atlantic
himself, he penned those lyrics as a tribute to a mighty
God who can comfort the soul in any disaster. He
would go on to found a ministry in Jerusalem that
would help save hundreds of lives during World War I.

It's funny, or maybe miraculous, depending on
how you look at things, that God will bring a song into
your life at a moment when you need it most. I was
attending church one Sunday during our most

tumultuous days and during the "praise and worship" time, someone sang the Casting Crowns song "Praise You In This Storm." It's like a modern-day version of "It Is Well With My Soul." I probably had heard "Praise You In This Storm" before but never paid close attention to the lyrics. On this particular Sunday, my eyes filled with tears as they sang…

> *And I'll praise You in this storm*
> *And I will lift my hands*
> *For You are who You are*
> *No matter where I am*
> *And every tear I've cried*
> *You hold in Your hand*
> *You never left my side*
> *And though my heart is torn*
> *I will praise You in this storm*

Have you ever been in a situation where a life storm was threatening to take you under? To my wife and me, it seemed as though every aspect of our life, except maybe our marriage, was collapsing. When good friends and family asked, "How are you guys doing?" we had literally replied, "We are learning to praise God in the storm." When I heard those lyrics, I silently rejoiced because I knew God was speaking directly to us. Thanks Casting Crowns for writing a song just for us!

Praising God in difficult circumstances is one of the greatest lessons He teaches His children. It is a lesson we must learn, because some amount of suffering is inherent in every believer's life. This concept should not come as a surprise to Christians because Jesus Himself warned us that we would experience tribulation in John chapter 15:

"Remember the word that I said to you: 'A servant is not greater than his master.' If they persecuted me, they will also persecute you. If they kept my word, they will also keep yours. But all these things they will do to you on account of my name, because they do not know him who sent me." – John 15:20-21

Who will persecute us? The "world" will, if we identify with Jesus, but we also can expect attacks from Satan. If you are tracking closely with Christ and seeking to do His will, be prepared for suffering, and when you are suffering, fight back with worship.

Some Christians become angry when they experience life challenges, and I certainly did during some of our worst days. But why should we expect a perfect life when we live in a fallen world filled with sinful people (myself included)? Things go wrong all the time, bad things happen to good people and Satan is grateful for any opportunity to drive a wedge between us and our Heavenly Father. Our own human nature often exacerbates the problem. We somehow think that we are naturally righteous and God should be continually rewarding us for our good behavior.

Hey Lord, look, I tithe my income and I've been on four short-term mission trips! Can I have a new boat now? Subconsciously I still think this way. I have to work hard to remind myself that, in reality, I am a self-absorbed sinner and my very best behavior, when compared to a Holy God, is no better than filthy rags. I also must understand that if I am to grow and become more like Jesus, suffering is an essential part of my development. This is no secret to anyone who reads much Scripture.

"Count it all joy, my brothers, when you meet trials of various kinds, for you know that the testing of your faith produces steadfastness. And let stead-fastness have its full effect, that you may be perfect and complete, lacking in nothing." – James 1:2-4

In suffering we attain greater unity with Christ. We can empathize with His pain on the cross as He empathizes with us in our agony. One of the most emotional moments I experienced during our ordeals was a time when, in a moment of grieving over my family, I said to myself, "God, why have you forsaken me?" I immediately remembered Jesus' words on the cross and began weeping. I am not worthy to suffer like Jesus, but in that moment I felt closer to Jesus than at perhaps any time in my life. We also develop greater unity with other believers when they suffer. A crisis is never fun, but suffering helps us identify with others who are hurting and it can change our eternal perspective (more on that later.)

I don't know if music will soothe a savage beast, but it will soothe a troubled soul. The effect of a praise song on someone who is suffering emotional pain is like an antacid to heartburn; it makes you feel better almost instantly, even if only for a short time. For that reason, I keep a list of favorite praise songs in my desk (along with some antacids), and on really grim days I can Google one of those songs and get relief for a few moments. People who read music and play instruments must have a great advantage when they are depressed. They can make a joyful noise to the Lord without incurring the scorn of family and pets. Me? I have to hum quietly.

One of my favorite songs when I was in college was a country song by Mac Davis called "It's Hard To Be Humble." It's amazing that I like this song because I am actually a rhythm and blues fan who typically hates country music. Nevertheless, this song is special because it accurately expresses an emotion that is common to everyone – unabated pride. I vividly remember the chorus of drunken college boys bellowing the lyrics near the end of many a frat party. The song reflects how we often feel about ourselves when we forget that God is actually the One who is in charge.

Oh, Lord, it's hard to be humble

The Peace Equation

When you're perfect in every way
I can't wait to look in the mirror
'Cause I get better lookin' each day

To know me is to love me
I must be a hell of a man
Oh, Lord, it's hard to be humble
But I'm doin' the best that I can

September 6, 2011

Dear Lefty,

It is painful to raise boys. I am learning that lesson a little bit every day. As your brother Rainey gets older, he gets bigger and stronger and more mature. This creates all sorts of problems.

For one thing, I don't want to wrestle any more. I'm 54 and tired. Nevertheless, he sometimes gets a "wrestling jones" and jumps on me, then the fight is on! I'm still stronger than he is and I outweigh him by 40 pounds. I can usually get him in a hold and lay on top of him, but he keeps struggling and biting and pinching 'til I wear out and let him up. Then, it starts all over again. The other night our battle lasted for at least 15 minutes of very strenuous tussling. It started in our bedroom and ended in the living room with Haley admonishing Rainey to "Stop, he's old and you're gonna break him!" It took me at least 15 minutes to catch my breath after that battle. I thought I was having a heart attack.

I never had a broken bone in my life until Rainey came along. By last count, I've now had four, maybe five broken bones — two ribs, a hand, and two fingers. One of these days he's going to put me in the hospital. On the night he broke my ribs I actually thought I might die. I was in so much discomfort I could barely breathe. I laid propped up in a chair with pillows all night trying to sleep. I told your mother when she went to bed to get up during the night and check on me, in case my breathing stopped. I'm serious!

A few weeks ago I went out to play catch with him in the street. We use this time for him to practice his pitching with me acting as his catcher. You know how hard he throws, right? One of the pitches was low and skipped off the pavement, right into my left ankle. The pain was excruciating. Took me five minutes to walk it off. I didn't want to cry or quit, lest I set a bad example for him, so I crouched down again and continued the workout. Three pitches later the same thing happened, except to my right ankle. I threw down my baseball glove and limped around pitifully for 10 minutes before declaring, "I quit." Both ankles were swollen and bruised the next day and I had trouble walking for a week.

Of course, the injuries listed here are just a sampling of many ways he has hurt me. You remember the time he hit me in the back of the head with a baseball? When he was little, he would sometimes grab my nose (hard to miss, I know) and try to rip it off, his razor-claw fingernails tearing my skin. How many times has he hit me in the groin? I'm unable to have children now! Thank goodness for that, cause another boy would surely kill me.

Love,
Dad

Chapter 6 The power of prayer

"I have been driven many times upon my knees by the overwhelming conviction that I had nowhere else to go. My own wisdom and that of all about me seemed insufficient for that day." – Abraham Lincoln

When my kids were small we used to encourage them to lead us in prayer before meals. Tracy and I felt it was a good way to teach them the importance of prayer and give them confidence to pray in front of others. The great thing about children is they don't feel the need to be sanctimonious or use big words to impress others seated around the table. Children keep things simple. That's why we have the classic kids' mealtime prayer, "God is great, God is good. Let us thank Him for our food. Amen." Brief and eloquent, and when you break it down, it covers a lot of theological ground – the majesty of God, His righteousness, our thankfulness for his provision... not bad for fourteen words. However, this wonderful and concise prayer proved too much for my son when he was four. Hungry and eager to get started, his mealtime prayer was, "I love pickles. Amen!"

He has become more eloquent over the years.

We let kids pray small prayers because they don't yet understand the greatness of God, His mercy and provision, and all the other attributes we learn as we mature in our faith. However, there are many adult believers who never mature past infancy in their prayer life. They may be faithful church attenders, teachers, even leaders, but they still pray puny prayers when they approach the Master. This was true of me for many years. I treated our Heavenly Father and Almighty God as a vending machine, going to him for favors and needs, attempting to push the right button to get what I wanted, typically something to do with health, safety and prosperity for me and my loved ones. I wasn't really concerned with what God wanted (He wanted my heart and affection). I prayed for others, but only as an act of duty, not with real love. I didn't pray for God to shape my heart to be like His. I didn't pray for God to be glorified. I usually took some time to thank God for His blessings, but only in the way you thank a waiter for serving your meal; I try to be polite but, after all, it is their job.

In his book, *The Prayer Of Jesus*, author Hank Hanegraaff, writes about our attitude toward prayer. "Prayer is not a magic formula to get things from God. Communicating with God in prayer is itself the prize.[10]" For a genuine follower of Jesus, what could be more important, or better, than a conversation with God The Father? During my years in the advertising and marketing business, we would go to great lengths for an opportunity to meet an important business leader or CEO. Access to powerful people is often vital to personal success. Yet, as Christians, we sometimes think of prayer as a tedious obligation, a box to check on our holy "to do" list. Prayer should be considered one of the greatest privileges of the Christian life. Thanks to Jesus, we can have an audience any time we choose with the Creator of the universe. Add to that the thought that no one anywhere at any time loves you more than God does. Your biggest advocate and the lover of your soul is always available for a meeting, and you have a personal assistant, the Holy Spirit, to help facilitate the discussion.

Unfortunately, our conversations with God are often little more than a shopping list of needs with the bookends of "Dear Heavenly Father" and "In Jesus name I pray." One of the great benefits of trials and tribulation is that our prayers often get much more intense and sincere. "Fervent" is a word I often hear associated with serious prayer. The word means "having or displaying passionate intensity." There is nothing like a personal emergency to make our prayer life more passionate and intense. Instead of praying, "Dear Lord, bless my kids," I got very specific and practical with God. "Please help my daughter fight her addiction today, and help her recall all of the Biblical principles she learned over the years, and protect her from temptation..." For my business I prayed, "Lord, help us meet our financial obligations today, and give us wisdom to make good decisions so that our company will survive and we can pay our employees, and please allow the checks from our clients to arrive soon." These prayers, I think, met the prayer guidelines laid out in James 4. This passage describes a right relationship with God in prayer. It tells us that we often pray but do not receive because we ask wrongly, with improper motives. It tells us to "draw near to God and He will draw near to you." It reminds us to humble ourselves before the Lord. In my darkest days of 2011-2013, my prayer life became alive and fresh. I was humble before the Lord (I certainly had no reason to boast), I was specific in my requests and I prayed often that God would deliver me so that I could give Him the glory. During that time and since then, I found that my conversations with God were devoid of the rote language that had I previously used. I considered every private prayer time, and there were many of them, to be crucial because so much was at stake.

I specifically recall a day during one of my daughter's rehab stints when my wife and I went to visit her. The facility was a three-hour drive from home. Normally, we would have spent the time chatting or listening to the radio, but this was a critical time in my daughter's treatment. She was floundering in her recovery and had the option to either stay or leave; she was a voluntary patient. If she stayed, we assumed she would continue to get better. If she chose to leave, then she was, *de facto*, choosing heroin addiction over sobriety. These were desperate times. We took turns praying for her as we drove, pouring out our hearts to God. There were no "prayer clichés" in our pleas, only the honest cries of two parents who wanted to see their daughter healed. Few times in my life have I been more passionate or humble when praying. There were lots of passionate prayers during this time – for my little girl, for my other kids, for my business and for my church. My relationship with the Lord grew more real and more intimate. It's very much like watching a friendship grow through candid and real conversation. I got very honest with God and admitted some of the character sins I had never before acknowledged: pride, selfishness, anger, impatience and a lack of genuine faith. He let me know He was listening and He cared. The recovery process, for my daughter, my business and me, was slower than I would have liked, but we were on God's timing and he was teaching us patience. For the record, my daughter stayed in rehab that day, which was a huge relief and definitely an answer to prayer. She later relapsed and was kicked out, but that is a whole other prayer story. God gave us what we and our daughter needed that day.

Another wonderful outcome from our season of discontent was the outpouring of prayer support from our family and friends. From the very moment we found out about our daughter's addiction we called on our loved ones and asked them to start praying. I take to heart the advice offered in James 5:16,

"Therefore, confess your sins to one another and pray for one another, that you may be healed. The prayer of a righteous person has great power as it is working."

There is great power in the prayers of righteous believers. I know a lot of incredible Christians, and I wanted them all praying on our behalf. I made phone calls and sent emails. We were not too proud to share our problems and ask these saints to intercede for us. I am humbled to know these spiritual giants were speaking to Jehovah on our behalf.

In times of great despair, you may find it hard to know what to pray. Sometimes there are life circumstances that offer no clear solution or direction. Such was the case in 2000. My elderly mother suffered a stroke and was unable to swallow. The doctors assured us this was an irreversible condition. My five siblings and I were faced with a difficult choice; authorize the doctors to put in a feeding tube, or don't authorize it and watch my mother starve to death. For some families, this would be an easy decision, but we all knew our mother's wishes; she did not want to be kept alive without some quality of life, and she was more than ready to go to Jesus and be reunited with loved ones in heaven. The thought of watching her wither away with no nourishment over many days or even weeks was agonizing. So we prayed, though we didn't know what to pray for. We simply asked for God's wisdom and for His best for our beloved Mother. We made the difficult decision to not insert a feeding tube and prayed that God, and our mom, would forgive us if we were in error. About a day later God delivered a miracle – against all medical odds, Mother regained her ability to swallow. Although she was unconscious most of the time and only able to swallow sips of liquids, she was getting nutrition. Mercifully, she passed easily into eternity several days later, and her children were spared the heartbreak of watching her suffer malnutrition.

The lesson here is, if you don't know what to pray, simply pray for God's best.

"And when you pray, do not heap up empty phrases as the Gentiles do, for they think that they will be heard for their many words. Do not be like them, for your Father knows what you need before you ask him." Matthew 6:7-8

A suggestion when you are troubled in spirit – reflective prayer.

Our church counselor, Dr. Bill Bellican, suggested this method of praying when you are dispirited and troubled. It's called reflective prayer. The idea is to use a specific piece of Scripture, usually one of the Psalms, and appropriate the words as if they are your own. On his blog site, Bill suggests the following steps:

- Get a translation of the Bible you enjoy.
- As you read a passage or Psalm, ask the Holy Spirit to open your mind and awareness to what He wants you to notice.
- Use a highlighter or pen to note the words, phrases or paragraphs that resonate with you. The Holy Spirit will bring these to your attention.
- Ask the Lord to enlighten your heart and soul regarding what He wants to teach you.
- When you have finished the entire passage, focus your attention on just the highlighted parts. Personalize and apply these portions to your own situation and honestly reflect your feelings and words to the Lord. You will

94

be telling Him, in light of the words you have highlighted, how you are affected, what you can or cannot do, and the struggles and tensions you are suffering.

- Ask the Holy Spirit to reveal new truth, provide peace and give direction.
- Be still and listen for His answer, and don't be discouraged if the answer does not come immediately – God works in His own timing.

95

The Peace Equation

September 7, 2011

Dear Lefty,

Oh chocolate, how do I love thee? Let me count the ways.
I love thee more than vanilla, strawberry or caramel, which also are delicious.
My mouth can taste the richness of a Hershey's Kiss
And the decadent goodness of a Reese's or Snickers.
Dark and milk chocolate, they fight for my affection,
And marshmallow with any chocolate is sublime!
This craving is part of my genetic make up,
A chromosome given me from the Halbrooks.
I cannot fight against this urging for chocolate,
Though my waistline strains against my belt.
I love you, chocolate, and you love me back;
You melt warmly in my mouth til I am satisfied.
You've brought smiles to me all my life, and if God Choose,
I shall but love thee better after death.

My ode to chocolate, with apologies to Elizabeth Barrett Browning.

Browning? Think I'll go eat a brownie!

Love,
Dad

Chapter 7 The comfort of counseling

"It's not that they can't see the solution. They can't see the problem." - G.K. Chesterton

Shiloh National Military Park is a Civil War battlefield located less than two hours from my home in Memphis. As a history buff, I've always enjoyed visiting there. It is a reverent and beautiful place, with peach orchards, meadows and some nice views of the Tennessee River. "Shiloh" is a Hebrew word that means "place of peace." It's ironic because on April 6, 1862, it was the site of the most violent and deadly battle ever fought on American soil up to that time. There were more than 23,000 casualties at Shiloh, a number almost equal to the casualties incurred during the entirety of the Revolutionary War. Americans at the time were appalled at the carnage. Before the war ended in 1865, there would be at least seven battles bloodier than Shiloh.

It is estimated that 620,000 men died during the Civil War, far more than any other American conflict.

By comparison, "only" 405,000 Americans died in World War II. What is often overlooked when examining the casualty figures of the Civil War is that most of them died of diseases. Despite the ferocity of the fighting, the canons and the rifled guns, the most dangerous enemies were germs. Approximately two-thirds of the deaths during the Civil War were due to disease. There was very little understanding of bacteria at the time. Sanitation issues, insects and poor nutrition helped to spread pathogens, as did the close proximity of the soldiers living in military camps. Many men from rural areas died from mumps, measles and other childhood diseases because they had not developed immunity to those ailments as children.

As we look back, we now see that the biggest threat was not combat, it was the battle going on inside them.

In times of great personal struggle – divorce, bankruptcy, drug dependency, serious illness – we may seek counseling from experts. We often think of counselors as physicians; we go to them for healing. What we find out is that the problem we can see is not the problem that is creating our anguish. For Christians, worry, stress and anxiety are usually the result of faulty faith. It is an internal, not external, issue. The battle may be raging around us, but our greatest enemy is the negative thinking that is raging in our mind. It is the kind of thinking that can lead a devoted Jesus follower to absolute despair, and maybe worse.

The word "counselor" can mean different things. There are professional counselors and psychologists who have special training and experience to help people cope with tough emotional, mental, psychological and spiritual issues – and sometimes these overlap. Psychiatrists are medical doctors who can prescribe drugs for people who need help dealing with severe mental health issues. Many Christians, me among them, also recognize the value of seeking help from mature believers whom we trust, someone who is wiser, more experienced and well-grounded in Scripture. In recent years I have gone to my friend Jay Robinson, one of our church elders and a man I admire very much. Jay is a retired arbitration attorney and a military vet with an Ivy League education. Not a bad resume. More importantly, he exudes kindness and walks closely with the Lord. It's very important to have people in your life who possess wisdom and are not afraid to tell you the truth. I firmly believe that the Lord can speak to us through the advice of the Godly men and women we know. It's one of the many benefits of belonging to a church – there are people there who can speak Biblical truth into your situation.

While I have never been reluctant to seek advice from mentors, until 2011 I had never gone to a professional counselor. My daughter's addiction, coupled with my business struggles and other life issues had put both Tracy and me into a precarious mental state. Fortunately, our church has a full-time Christian psychological counselor with years of experience. Within days of discovering Jordan's addiction, we called to schedule a meeting with him.

Dr. Bill Bellican has, in one sense, been a counselor nearly all his life. His father, an executive with the Holiday Inn Corporation, died when he was 13. Afterward, he became "something of a caretaker" to his emotionally needy mother. Although he had a natural curiosity about psychology and counseling, he resisted the urge to enter the field and instead went to work for his father's former company, Holiday Inn, in the area of customer service. This was at the height of the company's success, and Bill prospered for two decades. Although a Christian, his faith was anemic. "My attitude was, 'thanks, God. I'll call when I need you.'"

In 1991 Holiday Inn was purchased by a European company and shortly thereafter, Bill was laid off. It was time to call God.

"I was going to church in those days, but God was always on the back burner. When I was laid off, I assumed I would find another job quickly because I had a large network of friends and business associates and I had a very good resume. But all the promising job opportunities dried up. I was able to get some work as a consultant in customer service, but financially we were up and down. It was very stressful, and this went on for eight years. I look back on this time as my 'dark night of the soul.'"

Bill explained that the "dark night of the soul" was a phrase attributed to a Spanish guy named St. John of the Cross, who is not to be confused with St. John the apostle who was at the cross. If you Google "St. John of the Cross," you find that he was a major figure of the Counter-Reformation. You have to be a church history scholar to know much about the Counter-Reformation, and that's not important now. The important thing to know about St. John of the Cross is that he wrote a famous poem titled "The Dark Night of the Soul," which is about the bleak times in a Christian's life that God uses to shape and strengthen their character. That poem, or at least that topic, has resulted in many essays and books from famous theologians and psychologists such as R.C. Sproul, A.W. Tozer and S.Y. Tan. Apparently, the use of two initials is necessary to get into the smart Christians' club.

"The dark night of the soul... This is no ordinary fit of depression, but it is a depression that is linked to a crisis of faith, a crisis that comes when one senses the absence of God or gives rise to a feeling of abandonment by Him." R.C. Sproul

"It was during this time, this dark night of the soul, that God got my attention," said Bill. "I discovered over time what it was like to have a real relationship with God. Those dark days forced me to engage with God through His Word. There was a passage in Psalm 119 that had a profound impact on me. It clarified my understanding of God and gave me a new purpose."

Psalms 119:65-75

You have dealt well with your servant,
O LORD, according to your word.
Teach me good judgment and knowledge,
for I believe in your commandments.
Before I was afflicted I went astray,
but now I keep your word.
You are good and do good;
teach me your statutes.
The insolent smear me with lies,
but with my whole heart I keep your precepts;
their heart is unfeeling like fat,
but I delight in your law.
It is good for me that I was afflicted,
that I might learn your statutes.

"It says, 'before I was afflicted, I went astray.' Then it goes on to say, 'it was good for me that I was afflicted, that I might learn your statutes.' I began to realize that God had a calling on my life for more than 20 years, a call to counseling, but I had resisted it. I had always had a desire to help and counsel people, and

He used this encounter through Scripture to rekindle that desire. I realized that God loved me enough to afflict me so that I might experience His calling on my life."

Not long after this epiphany Bill enrolled in a program to obtain a master's degree in Christian counseling. He later earned a doctorate from Ashland Theological Seminary and has gone on to obtain numerous certifications and win many accolades, including the Servant Leadership Award for 2013 from the American Association of Christian Counselors. The association has 50,000 members. He has provided more than 22,000 hours of counseling, most of it through his ministry at Central Church in Memphis. All of his counseling is offered free of charge to members and non-members of the church.

Bill was incredibly kind and helpful to my wife and me when we were at our most vulnerable, and he provided some key insights to our faith and our thought process at just the time we needed new perspective. He recognized that we were going through our own dark night of the soul, and that God was trying to teach us something important. He also reminded us that even though our circumstances were horrible, God loved us and was still in control.

Bill's counseling, though gentle and wise, soothed my anxiety, but it did not eliminate it. After a session with Bill my worries would dissipate for a while, then, like an ocean tide, roll back in and torment me. It seemed a little bit like having the wheels aligned on your car. Bill, the experienced mechanic, would get me back in alignment with good advice and proper perspective, but after hitting a few potholes, my thinking would get wobbly and out of alignment again. After many weeks my tires began to wear thin and I was struggling to keep my mind out of the ditch, metaphorically speaking.

This is why Philippians 4:4-9 bothered me so much. In my mind, the peace that surpasses all understanding was hanging there like a carrot on a stick, but it seemed just out of my reach. The harder I struggled for it, the wearier and more defeated I felt. I began to think that peace would eventually come only if our daughter and my business both recovered, but in my heart I knew that this was not a correct Biblical attitude. Philippians 4:6-7 says:

"Do not be anxious about anything, but in everything by prayer and supplication with thanksgiving let your requests be made known to God. And the peace of God, which surpasses all understanding, will guard your hearts and your minds in Christ Jesus."

I was discussing this passage with a friend of mine and he pointed out that Philippians 4:7 is the only time the phrase "the peace of God" appears in the Bible. This phrase is not talking about *our* peace, it's referring to the peace "that belongs to God" or the peace "that comes from God." It surpasses our human understanding because it isn't OUR peace, it is HIS. It is God's peace that guards our hearts and minds. It is insurmountable because it belongs to HIM. He gives it to us. God's peace is bubble-wrap for our souls; it is Kevlar for our psyche. Since it belongs to God, it is completely reliable and trustworthy. The "peace of God" in Philippians 4:7, is a peace that only God possesses and only God can dispense to his children to help them handle the stress of their lives.

Thankfully, this peace does not depend on me and is not attained or maintained by me. Rather, it comes from God and envelops me when I "rejoice in the Lord always." It surrounds me when I let my requests be made known to God by prayer and supplication with thanksgiving. My relationship with Jesus Christ fills me with the Holy Spirit and the Spirit comforts with a powerful peace. It belongs to God and is given to us as a shield of protection against crippling worry, anxiety, and depression. It is present so long as we are focused on Jesus.

Emotional pain is natural and unavoidable sometimes, but it does not have to be overwhelming if we submit to the work of the Holy Spirit in our lives. Peace and patience are among the "fruit of the Spirit" that we receive at the time of our salvation, fruit that should be cultivated as our faith in God grows.

"But the fruit of the Spirit is love, joy, peace, patience, kindness, goodness, faithfulness, gentleness, self-control; against such things there is no law." Galatians 5:22

I am promised, by God no less, peace and patience, but in 2011-2013 I was rarely at peace, so obviously I was not enjoying the fruit of the Holy Spirit in my life. My peace was measured in minutes. Mostly I was miserable. I put the question of peace to my counselor, Bill Bellican. Why does God not remove my pain? I'm doing everything by the Book! God's protective peace seems to wash off like cheap sun block when I jump in the pool. He leaned back in his office chair. There was no hesitation in his answer; it was obviously a question he had addressed before.

"About 99 percent of the people I counsel want solutions to their problems, and there is nothing wrong with that; it's a natural reaction to the bad things that happen in life. But if we are believers, we must try to look at things from God's perspective. What is He trying to teach us? He wants us to see Himself as part of the solution. God's perspective transcends our circumstances."

Bill then said something that every Jesus follower must come to understand.

"Some people pray for protection all the time, or to have all their problems taken away. And again, there is nothing wrong with that. But God loves us too much to answer that prayer in the way we want Him to. We need to experience problems so our faith has a chance to grow, to know that we can count on Him when we cry out, 'Abba Father."

"Peace does not necessarily mean the absence of problems," he continued. "The peace that surpasses all understanding is peace that prevails in spite of problems."

Okay, I accept the premise that everyone has problems, and God can use my problems to help increase my faith. Nevertheless, that's of little comfort when you are depressed, stressed and worried. How do we move from chaos to calm, and stay there? As we learned previously, the "peace of God" which surpasses all understanding, the peace described in Philippians 4:7, is a peace that can only come from God. We cannot possess it, but He will protect us with it, like an umbrella on a rainy day. Think of God as holding the umbrella; when we are close to Him we remain warm and dry, protected from the storms of life. When we get too far away, we get wet and cold. The key is staying close to God through frequent and passionate prayer, living in the Word of God and "abiding in Christ," which is a churchy way of saying "stay connected," like grapes to a grape vine.

"I am the vine; you are the branches. Whoever abides in me and I in him, he it is that bears much fruit, for apart from me you can do nothing." John 15:5

It's important to note that maintaining a close relationship with Jesus requires some effort. Our natural tendency is to drift. "Prone to wander, Lord, I feel it!" Hymn writer Robert Robinson penned those words in 1758 and they are still true today. It takes constant effort to keep my eyes on Jesus. Otherwise, my gaze returns earthward, and when that happens, I slip back into the blues.

It can be very difficult to keep your eyes fixed on the Lord during a crisis. Think of hitting a tennis ball with angry hornets swarming around your head. Keeping a Christ-centered attitude can be nearly impossible, even for the strongest believers. The problem of losing focus on the Savior can become more acute the longer you are anxious or sad. At some point you begin to think there is no hope. There have been times when I felt that way – defeated. God wants us to be content in all circumstances, but my circumstances were too big.

Something Bill told us during our first visit stuck with me over the next two years and became something of a touchstone in my search for genuine peace. He said it near the end of our first session, as we were preparing to leave his office. "Don't miss the lesson God is trying to teach you." Those words reverberated with us for months afterward. It was essentially the question I had been asking – what lesson do I need to learn to achieve lasting peace? Why could

I not accept the challenges we were facing with the assurance and inner joy that God was going to take care of everything? What was wrong with my faith?

Bill's admonition to not miss the "lesson God was trying to teach us" became a compass on our faith journey. When we felt fearful or hopeless, we asked God to reveal his lesson for us. God's answer did not come during those darkest moments; it came later. During our suffering I questioned my faith, even my relationship with Jesus. Jehovah God was trying to teach me lessons about His character, but I was struggling to learn them. I knew I must be patient and wait on the Lord, but patience in suffering is mighty hard. I'm an American in the 21st Century. Why could I not just take a pill and have instant patience and faith?

"Developing faith through patience is a little like lifting weights to get stronger," Bill explained. "You have to enter into the process with the expectation that it will work. You have to patiently and persistently exercise, and maybe you don't notice you are getting stronger each time, but you are. A certain amount of pain and patience are necessary. Some people give up; that's why when you go to a fitness center in January, all the weight machines are in use, but go back in February and there are plenty of machines available. Developing real strength takes time and effort. The same is true with faith."

109

September 9, 2011

Dear Lefty,

100 Reasons I'm Glad I'm a Guy – Reason #2:
Childbirth

     I am the father of three children and have witnessed natural childbirth three times. Childbirth is a beautiful thing. Well, beautiful aside from the screaming... and the blood... and the placenta... and the cutting of the umbilical... and that "look" Tracy gave me during the most intense part of her labor. Otherwise, it's great.

     Honestly, I never wanted to be in the delivery room. I would have preferred to be in the waiting room smoking cigarettes, and I don't smoke. Like Prissy in "Gone With The Wind," I didn't know nothin' about birthin' no babies. Sure, I went to the classes with Tracy and tried to pay attention, but I really didn't retain very much knowledge. It was like that modern art class I took in college; I didn't think I actually had to know that stuff, I just needed credit for showing up. When it was zero hour in the hospital delivery room, I was completely unprepared for the shock and awe of birth.

     I have heard childbirth described in various ways. My favorite: it's like passing a watermelon through your nose. But it's not a watermelon and it's not your nose. It's messy, nerve wracking and not very dignified for the mother. Every time I see a delivery table and that apparatus for the legs, I'm grateful that the serpent got to Eve first.

Men love to show how tough they are. You've seen those shirtless dudes at football games in December with their chests painted and a bottle of Jack in their back pocket. Guys are constantly trying to prove their toughness. Mothers don't have to paint their chests; they can just point at their kids.

As for people who videotape childbirth, I have one word – don't. God gave us memories so we don't have to digitally record extremely private bodily functions that will embarrass, and gross out, our friends. I would rather watch endless reruns of "Say Yes To The Dress" than endure five minutes of childbirth video.

Let this be a warning to you, daughter.

Love,
Dad

Chapter 8 The Peace Equation: A beginning

You can learn a great deal by reading bumper stickers. My automobile carries only one message on its bumper – I am an Arkansas State University Red Wolf. We live in the South and the college you attended often tells more about you than your religious or political affiliation. Any other philosophical principles I have are left to the imagination of those who drive behind me. Nevertheless, I appreciate what people choose to reveal about themselves through bumper stickers. One of my all-time favorites was the message "Jesus is coming – look busy." That sums up the America Christian attitude, don't you think? Another favorite was "No God, no peace. Know God, know peace." It took me a few moments to unravel the philosophy communicated in those eight words, but when I got it, I had to applaud the writer for such a clever and powerful message. If you don't "know" God, how can you ever know peace in your soul? A simple, profound and effective statement.

That bumper sticker message crystalized the spiritual conflict I experienced in 2011-2013. I "knew" God both in an academic and personal sense; or as we evangelicals like to say, I had both "head and heart knowledge." As a believer for almost 50 years, I had many times examined and rehashed my relationship with Jesus and my "salvation experience." I am absolutely convinced that I love Jesus and had gratefully accepted His free gift of salvation. However, despite my assurance of His presence in my heart, I have often experienced periods of great stress and worry – in other words, a lack of peace. The Bible promises peace repeatedly in Scripture, even "peace that surpasses all understanding," but the peace I experienced was always fleeting. My mind was often embroiled in conflict and anxiety. This was especially true during the events that occurred in our lives in 2011-2013. I had such spiritual turmoil that I began to doubt my faith. It begged the question, why can't I find lasting peace in my mind and soul?

A sampling of the Bible's promises of peace:

"May the Lord give strength to his people! May the Lord bless his people with peace!" Psalms 29:11

"I will listen to what God the Lord will say; he promises peace to his people, his saints-- but let them not return to folly." Psalms 85:8

"Peace I leave with you; my peace I give to you. Not as the world gives do I give to you. Let not your

hearts be troubled, neither let them be afraid." John 14:27

"And the peace of God, which surpasses all understanding, will guard your hearts and your minds in Christ Jesus." Philippians 4:7

"Jesus said to them again, "Peace be with you. As the Father has sent me, even so I am sending you." John 20:21

"I have told you these things, so that in me you may have peace. In this world you will have trouble. But take heart! I have overcome the world." John 16:33

"Now may the Lord of peace himself give you peace at all times and in every way. The Lord be with all of you." 2 Thessalonians 3:16

Stress and anxiety often ebb and flow in a believer's life based on life's circumstances. This should not be, because our peace *should* be grounded in God's love and promises. Theoretically, we should maintain a consistent state of peace and tranquility in our minds and hearts. However, it is natural for humans, and even believers, to panic in times of stress. Remember Peter after he climbed out of the boat in Matthew 14. When he realized he was walking on rough seas and took his eyes off of the Lord, he began to sink. Job, in his misery, argued with God. Abraham, when faced with potential enemies, lied and told them his wife was his sister (dude, really?).

Stress and anxiety in the heart of a believer is not uncommon, but it is not what God wants for His children.

During our months of personal struggle, I combed the Scriptures for passages that spoke to my despair. I listened to uplifting praise music, I sought the counsel of Godly people, I prayed "fervently." I experienced brief periods of peace but I soon slumped back into depression and anxiety. The "what ifs" of my life situations came back to haunt me. What was I missing? The promise of peace was, for me, the paradox of peace.

My situation reminded me of Jacob wrestling with a "man" in Genesis 32. Jacob was experiencing serious stress. He was on his way to visit his brother Esau. Earlier in Genesis we are told that Jacob tricked his father into giving him Esau's birthright. Esau, a big, strapping outdoorsman, had threatened to kill his younger brother. After many years apart, Jacob was headed back to his homeland where he had to face Esau. Based on what we read in Scripture, Jacob was consumed with the "what ifs." What if Esau is still angry after all this time? What if he wants to destroy me and my entire family? Jacob prayed fervently (which, as we know, means "having or displaying passionate intensity")...

"O God of my father Abraham and God of my father Isaac, O Lord who said to me, 'Return to your

country and to your kindred, that I may do you good, I am not worthy of the least of all the deeds of steadfast love and all the faithfulness that you have shown to your servant, for with only my staff I crossed this Jordan, and now I have become two camps. Please deliver me from the hand of my brother, from the hand of Esau, for I fear him, that he may come and attack me, the mothers with the children. But you said, 'I will surely do you good, and make your offspring as the sand of the sea, which cannot be numbered for multitude.'" Genesis 32:9-12

That very night Jacob wrestled with God (likely the pre-incarnate Christ). The Biblical account says they wrestled all night, and the man could not overcome Jacob. Yet, at the crack of dawn, the man merely touches Jacob's thigh and dislocates his hip. Even after this orthopedic mishap Jacob demanded a blessing from the angel, which proves two things: Jacob was extremely stubborn and one very tough hombre. The man relented and blessed Jacob, then changed his name to Israel. The passage tells us that Jacob named the place where this took place "Peniel," which means, "I have seen God face to face, and yet my life has been delivered."

Like Jacob, God has repeatedly blessed me over my lifetime. But also like Jacob, when faced with new adversity, I become afraid and beg for help. When deliverance is uncertain, I wrestle with God,

116

urging Him, pleading with Him, to save me. My weak faith led me to ask questions such as, "God, I have been faithful to You for many years – why have you turned Your back on me? Why is my daughter being punished with addiction? Why did You not protect us from Satan? I followed Your Word in raising my kids, so why are they suffering? Why is my business in trouble? Why is my boy disappointed and discouraged? Why God?"

This question of faith was especially troubling. I HAD faith. I believed in God with all my heart. Of course, I was fully aware of James 2:19 (NIV), *"You believe that there is one God. Good! Even the demons believe that—and shudder."* I *had* accepted Christ as my personal Lord and Savior. I had no doubt of that. Therefore, I should have peace that surpasses all understanding...right? Yet, I did not. My frustration was compounded when I read passages such as Matthew 7:7-10:

"Ask, and it will be given to you; seek, and you will find; knock, and it will be opened to you. For everyone who asks receives, and the one who seeks finds, and to the one who knocks it will be opened. Or which one of you, if his son asks him for bread, will give him a stone? Or if he asks for a fish, will give him a serpent? If you then, who are evil, know how to give good gifts to your children, how much more will your Father who is in heaven give good things to those who ask him!"

I was asking, seeking and knocking. I was receiving *some* peace, but it was always short-lived. Was God giving me a serpent when I asked for a fish? Why did I not have perpetual peace? Perhaps I was just the typical American "consumer Christian." In an age of social media and fast food, I've come to expect immediate gratification. Why is the microwave oven so slow? The ice dispenser in the refrigerator door takes forever! I've wasted half my life waiting for hot water from the faucet! God, I prayed about this yesterday; where's my relief?

My, how impatient we are when God is attempting to teach us important lessons!

"Wait on the Lord; be of good courage, and He shall strengthen your heart; Wait, I say, on the Lord!" Psalms 27:14

I remembered the advice of our church counselor, Bill Bellican, "Don't let the lessons God is trying to teach you go to waste." What I failed to realize, and what was so hard for me to accept, is this: important lessons take *time* to learn. You don't learn calculus in a day. That knowledge is built over many years. You first must learn to count. Later you learn long division and fractions. Then comes algebra and geometry. Then you are perhaps ready for calculus. This was how God taught me about the deeper level of faith that He desires for us; not the superficial consumer-Christian, happy times country-club-church

118

faith, but the type of faith you learn by relying on God and battling your enemy, the devil, on a daily, sometimes hourly, basis. That type of faith is built layer upon layer, and in my case, the lessons took 50 years. By 2011, I was ready for the advanced course, which took three years to complete. God was teaching me about *sanctifying* faith – a level of confidence in God that develops over time as we learn to trust Him in every situation, even the really tough ones. It is the kind of confidence that Whitney Clay learned when she lost her daughter before she ever held her in her arms. It was the confidence Sherry Welch understood when she buried her husband and father in the same month while she was undergoing cancer treatments herself.

Seminary graduates call this "progressive sanctification." Patience in God is necessary to develop sanctifying faith. James 5 talks about the connection between suffering and patience, and how the Lord blesses those who are steadfast (patient).

"Be patient, therefore, brothers, until the coming of the Lord. See how the farmer waits for the precious fruit of the earth, being patient about it, until it receives the early and the late rains. You also, be patient. Establish your hearts, for the coming of the Lord is at hand... As an example of suffering and patience, brothers, take the prophets who spoke in the name of the Lord. Behold, we consider those blessed

who remained steadfast. You have heard of the steadfastness of Job, and you have seen the purpose of the Lord, how the Lord is compassionate and merciful." James 5:1-8, 10-11

According to James, even the ancient prophets were required to endure suffering to learn patience. For me suffering was necessary, and the link between suffering and patience is a necessary step in God's sanctification process for his children.

It's important to note that patience is one of the "fruits of the Spirit." We receive the Holy Spirit when we become followers of Jesus. Galatians 5:22-23 tells us the fruit of the spirit is love, joy, peace, <u>patience</u>, kindness, goodness, faithfulness, gentleness and self-control. As our relationship with Jesus grows, the fruits of the Spirit become more evident in our lives. How does our relationship with the Father grow? Studying the Word and Scripture memorization can help. You also grow through fellowship with mature believers, as well as worship and prayer. But perhaps the most powerful growth tool is suffering.

Suffering! No way. Being a Christian is all about prayers (if they're not too long), praise songs, communion and two-week mission trips. Christians don't experience real suffering, right? I mean, who would sign up for the whole Jesus gig if suffering were part of the agreement? But if you read the fine print (the Bible), it's there in black and white. Peter, the rock of the church, was in Rome where Nero was burning Christians to light the streets at night. The book of 1 Peter is his letter to persecuted believers everywhere.

"Beloved, do not be surprised at the fiery trial when it comes upon you to test you, as though something strange were happening to you. But rejoice insofar as you share Christ's sufferings, that you may also rejoice and be glad when his glory is revealed… Therefore let those who suffer according to God's will entrust their souls to a faithful Creator while doing good." 1 Peter 4:12-13, 19

He's telling us that suffering, which would include anxiety, stress, grief, worry and depression, should be reason for rejoicing because suffering can be used to enhance our fellowship with Jesus. He goes on to write that we can "entrust our souls to a faithful Creator." God knows about grief and loss and He can be trusted to provide the comfort we need, as we need it. He watched His own son suffer terribly, and He watches us suffer. Why would a loving God just sit there (if, in fact, God needs to sit) and allow us to suffer? Because suffering may be the only motivation that will lead us to cling to Him. He wants an intimate relationship with us, but we typically don't embrace God until we are desperate. It's like Bill Bellican said, "Thanks God. I'll call you when I need you." We often do not value our relationship with God until we are

121

tested. He is the pearl of great value, and having an abiding relationship with Him is worth everything (Matthew 13:45-46).

I was beginning to understand that having God's peace is a process. The process includes *patience* in times of suffering, and patience is not learned in a moment, it is a virtue that is developed over a period of time. Remaining steadfast (patient) during life's challenges and trusting God to deliver us in times of trouble builds our *confidence* in Him. We must learn to trust God's promises and be confident that He will comfort us through all afflictions.

> *"When the righteous cry for help, the LORD hears*
> *and delivers them out of all their troubles.*
> *The LORD is near to the brokenhearted*
> *and saves the crushed in spirit.*
> *Many are the afflictions of the righteous,*
> *but the LORD delivers him out of them all."*
> Psalms 34:17-19

Faith + patience + confidence = peace. Is this God's formula for peace? It sounds simple enough in theory, but there seemed to be a big unknown variable in this linear equation. All the patience in the world and supreme confidence in God doesn't always help if you cannot see an end to your suffering. The quadriplegic who is helpless and lonely; the single mom whose teenage son commits suicide; the man who is convicted and sentenced to life in prison... can they enjoy unsurpassed peace? Their pain will last a lifetime.

Let's remember that even Jesus's disciples did not have peace all the time; they doubted and despaired after the crucifixion because they thought all hope was lost. However, at some point, their anxiety evaporated and they became spiritual giants who went out and, against great persecution, founded the Church. They gave their lives willingly, peacefully, even joyfully for the cause of Christ.

So what changed for those guys? Seeing the resurrected Jesus and receiving the Holy Spirit were certainly big factors in developing their *confidence*. Seeing the resurrected Jesus would certainly build confidence. I believe in the resurrected Jesus, too, but my peace isn't always so great. In fact, my emotions often tip to despair when the weight of anxiety becomes heavier than my hope. I have sometimes worried that my troubles would never end, that despair is unavoidable, like taxes and death. Obviously, my understanding of the Peace Equation was somehow incomplete. I was still missing something.

October 10, 2011

Dear Lefty,

I have seen and experienced many wonderful things in my life and I want to list some of them here. Let's get some of the obvious ones out of the way first – seeing your mother walk down the aisle in her wedding dress, seeing my three babies for the first time. Playing with my kids on Christmas mornings. Those were awesome and indelible memories, but here are a few more moments I consider highlights of my life.

- *Standing on a mountain in Nepal looking at the Himalayas. I could not get over the idea that a poor boy from Tucker, Arkansas, was looking at one of the most magnificent sights in the whole world.*

- *Seeing your mother, eight months pregnant, do a perfect front roll then spring to her feet while chasing the neighbors' little dog in our front yard. Every few years Tracy does something that absolutely amazes me.*

- *Finding the "first place" sign in our front yard when we won the neighborhood Christmas lights decorating contest. I was totally shocked that we won – still am.*

- *As a kid with your Aunt Sandra and Uncle Herman at the circus, I saw an enormous tiger pee on a woman wearing a fur coat.*

- *Sitting on a soccer field in Xian, China, at midnight praying with two students to receive Christ. I had asked God to give me the experience of leading someone to Him, and He did!*

- *Waiting with you to walk down the aisle at your wedding, listening to the bagpiper, then hearing Rev. Josh Ramsay said, "Now that's the way to make an entrance!"*

- *Standing with my brother and sisters at my mother's bedside as she died. Sounds like a sad time, but it was really triumphant, especially when you consider it was the first time all six of us siblings had been together at one place in 25 years. Only God could have orchestrated such a thing. I think it was a reward to my mother for being the spiritual foundation of our family for so many years.*

- *Walking into the Christmas Story house in Cleveland, Ohio, and seeing the leg lamp in the window. I felt like Ralphie on Christmas morning!*

- *Seeing you, Haley and Rainey's faces when we pulled up at the airport and explained that we were flying to Disneyworld and not driving to grandma's house! Totally surprised you!*

125

Here's to wonderful memories! May you have a thousand of these in your lifetime.

Love,
Dad

Chapter 9 My EUREKA! moment

Post-it® Notes are an incredible invention. So simple yet so useful. How Post-It® Notes were invented has a bit of divine inspiration behind it. According to the story a 3M scientist, Dr. Spencer Silver, developed a weak adhesive in 1968 that at first was thought to have no practical use. Several years later, another 3M scientist, Arthur Fry, became annoyed that the bookmarks he used in his church hymnal kept falling out. He remembered the weak adhesive created by Silver and had the idea of using it on his bookmarkers. It was strong enough to adhere without falling out of the hymnal yet it did not damage the pages when removed. After some consumer research and product development, 3M introduced Post It® Notes in 1979. Today, my desk is covered in sticky notes.

My "eureka!" moment was similar in that I had the solution to my peace problem for some time before I learned to apply it properly. I knew that faith, patience, confidence and peace were somehow connected, but the connection did not seem to produce the right result for me. At 2 a.m., on March 24, 2014, my Heavenly Father began revealing to me the missing variable I needed to experience the unsurpassed peace that I so badly wanted. My wrestling match with the Lord was coming to a conclusion, though I didn't realize it. He was still teaching me patience, how to seek the deeper truths of God, and as He had on numerous times before, God brought me back to the promise of Philippians 4:

"Rejoice in the Lord always; again I will say, rejoice. Let your reasonableness be known to everyone. The Lord is at hand; do not be anxious about anything, but in everything by prayer and supplication with thanksgiving let your requests be made known to God. And the peace of God, which surpasses all understanding, will guard your hearts and your minds in Christ Jesus."

The Holy Spirit led me to focus on the word *rejoice*, but I hardly felt like rejoicing. I had recently quit the highest-paying job I've ever had with no alternative plan in mind. Now I was worried about what would come next. I was uncertain and fearful. I wanted to rejoice, but instead was filled with anxiety. I felt lost. The Jews wandered in the wilderness for 40 years. In 40 years I would be 97! I didn't want to wait that long for God's promise.

As I lay in the dark and stared at the ceiling, I considered the possible consequences of my recent career move. I had deserted my friend and business partner and now had no means of income; we would have to live off our savings until God revealed His plan for us. What if nothing else came along? What if a health crisis occurred? What kind of example was I setting for my kids? Their dad is a quitter! Does all of this worry mean that I am mentally unstable? Maybe I am cracking up. Be patient and wait on the Lord, I reminded myself. But what if? It seemed as though I was in a spiritual straight jacket, struggling to be free of anxiety and fear.

Unable to sleep and near the edge of panic, the Holy Spirit whispered, "get up and go to your office." C'mon God, it's 2 a.m.! Fortunately, my office is upstairs in my house, so the command did not seem as drastic as God's directive to Abraham, *"Go from your country and your kindred and your father's house to the land that I will show you."* Given the comparison, going upstairs seemed reasonable to me. In my office, I sat at my computer, stared at the monitor and simply began to type. Within 30 minutes God revealed to me another vital missing ingredient in His equation for spiritual peace.

There, in the quiet of my office, the Holy Spirit reminded me of the difficult journey we had made over the past three years and how He had literally walked with us through the wilderness, often helping us make it from day to day by providing manna in the form of Scripture, a praise song or word of encouragement from a friend. He reminded me of the many life principles and promises He has given us... *Train up a child in the way he should go; even when they are old they will not depart from it* (Prov. 22:6), *I will never leave you nor forsake you* (Heb. 13:5), *My grace is sufficient for you, for My power is made perfect in weakness* (2 Cor. 12:9), and many, many more. He reminded me of Bill Bellican's admonition to not waste these wonderful lessons from God. He reminded me again to *rejoice*. There's that word again – rejoice. I can't rejoice; why should I? From my perspective my life seemed miserable.

From my perspective... The phrase rattled around in my head annoyingly, like a marble in a coffee mug. I remembered something else Bill Bellican said: "God's perspective transcends our circumstances." My own perspective seemed very bleak; we live our lives in a fallen world of broken hearts and dreams, illness and dying, depression and fear. That's how I saw things, but how does God see our human condition? What does life – specifically MY life – look like from His perspective? I think God sees my life, my story, as just beginning. If I take His eternal perspective, my five decades are like a nanosecond – one-billionth of a second – compared to eternity. Eternity is a concept we humans can barely fathom, for we have no experience with something that is not restrained

130

by time. The personal challenges we face, like illness, addiction, bankruptcy and death, can make life seem interminable, but it is not. James 4:14 describe life as "a vapor that appears for a little while and then vanishes away." The philosopher Ferris Bueller said, "Life goes by pretty fast. If you don't stop and look around once in a while, you could miss it." So true, it does go by very fast. However, when we are suffering through a painful experience, a day can seem like a year, and that creates a conundrum. Is life really short, or is it actually a long, painful slog? It is, I think, a matter of perspective.

When we were in the worst days of our daughter's addiction and my business problems seemed overwhelming, our days were long and painful; the weeks seemed like months. Our situation was exacerbated by the fact that we did not know what the outcome would be, nor when our circumstances would improve... or get worse. We were in a perpetual state of anxiety about the future, and anxiety makes time feel like a lead overcoat. What we failed to remember was the promise of Romans 8:28.

"And we know that for those who love God all things work together for good, for those who are called according to his purpose."

All things, even the bad things, will ultimately turn out for the good of those who love God. Hey,

Apostle Paul, that's a bold statement! What if my daughter dies of an overdose? How can that be good?

Perspective... if only I could have seen our situation from God's eternal perspective! Our Father knows that the human experience is a vapor that vanishes quickly, like your breath on a cold morning. He also knows that life on Earth is a pathetic shadow of life in heaven. Consider the words of Billy Graham after the 9/11 attacks in 2001. Reverend Graham addressed a grieving nation in a memorial service at the National Cathedral. He said of those who had died in Christ, "many of those people who died this past week are in heaven right now and they wouldn't want to come back. It's so glorious and so wonderful.[11]" We often think of clinging to life as our highest priority. Life can be wonderful and it is a gift from God, but life on Earth is only a prelude to our perfect life in heaven with Jesus. Said another way, for Christians, death is not the worst thing that can happen. Even if our daughter had died of an overdose, I know that the pain of separation would be relatively brief (compared to eternity), God would have comforted us in our loss and we would eventually be with her again FOR ETERNITY. Furthermore, God could use us as guides for those who come behind us, struggling to find their way through the chaos of a life challenge like the death of a loved one. You see, the Father sees our ENTIRE life, from birth through eternity.

His perspective is not limited to the keyhole that is the misery we are now enduring. We can rejoice, or at least find peace, in all situations if our perspective is right.

We don't yet see things clearly. We're squinting in a fog, peering through a mist. But it won't be long before the weather clears and the sun shines bright! We'll see it all then, see it all as clearly as God sees us, knowing him directly just as he knows us! (1 Corinthians 13:12, The Message)

I was seeing things more clearly now; *perspective* is essential in the Peace Equation because the proper perspective enables us to be *confident* of God's promises. The cancer patient will be healed, though her complete healing may not occur until she is in heaven. The addict who knows Jesus as Savior will be free of addiction, either in this world or the next. The paralyzed war veteran will walk again. Families will be reunited. God will wipe away all tears and alleviate all sadness. Our loving Father simply says, "Trust Me," but having confidence in Him doesn't always come easily.

I can honestly say He has always delivered me through every life challenge, but He often did so in unexpected ways. An example: My dad was diagnosed with cancer when he was 52 years old. I was 14. Until that time, he had been completely disinterested in God, despite my mother's prayers. He never went to church and he disdained Christians. His cancer diagnosis changed his attitude about God. He found a new interest in spiritual things. He eventually was saved, baptized and even sang solos in church (turns out he had a great voice). He built a new home for my mother and enjoyed four productive and happy years before he died in 1975. That was 40 years ago and I still miss him, but I know he's in heaven now. We have a lot of catching up to do when I get there, and I look forward to fishing with him (I believe there will be trout fishing in heaven). As it turns out, cancer was one of the best things that ever happened to him. You could say that it saved his life.

Confidence is an attitude that does not develop quickly; it takes time and the repeated faithfulness of God before the believer develops genuine sanctifying faith. Pairs figure skating – okay, all figure skating – bores me to death, but I do appreciate the relationship between the partners as they perform. The women, in particular, must have enormous confidence in their male partners because it is the female who often is hoisted or hurled into the air as they glide, sometimes backwards, on ice. That takes guts, and *confidence*, that the guy is going to be there when she comes down. The TV commentators often note that the two partners have worked diligently together for *years* to develop the chemistry and confidence necessary to perform these stunts. Typically, you don't develop full confidence in God as a new believer. It is only over time that you realize Jehovah Shammah (Hebrew phrase meaning "the Lord is there") is always there and always keeps His promises. Pretty soon you know that when life pitches you into the air, God will be there to catch you. This is sanctifying faith. Therefore...

Confidence = patience x time.

The Peace Equation – experiencing the peace that surpasses all understanding – was evolving into something that made sense to me.

• The process begins with saving faith – acknowledging your own sin and seeking the forgiveness of a loving Heavenly Father through faith in Jesus Christ. If you are not a follower of Jesus, the Peace Equation cannot work for you.

• Even if you are "saved," as evangelicals like to say, you need *confidence* that God's promises are absolutely reliable. That type of confidence must be chiseled into a Christian's heart by God over time through various trials, so *patience* over a period of *time* is necessary.

• If you have saving faith and confidence, you then must have the proper *perspective* – God's perspective. Life often does not make sense when we look at it from ground level. We need to see it from the Father's lofty position. We are eternal beings and life on this rock is just temporary.

135

Faith + *confidence* **+ Perspective = Peace!**

Eureka! This made sense to me. I could look at these variables and see that God's perfect peace is possible if I am a follower of Jesus Christ, learn patience through multiple life experiences, be confident in God's promises, and have a heavenly, eternal perspective. This is not a process I could know or do on my own. The Holy Spirit had to guide me through it. Like Jacob, I had wrestled with God, asking for His peace and His blessings. As I re-read that passage in Genesis, God illuminated verse 30, *"So Jacob called the name of the place Peniel, saying, 'For I have seen God face to face, and yet my life has been delivered.'"* It was *in the struggle* that Jacob saw God face-to-face. Just like Jacob, I'm still limping from my experiences over the past three years, but I encountered Jehovah in a new way, up close and personal. During my struggle – my suffering – I was unwilling to simply trust God with my future. He used stress and anxiety to break my hip, to humble me. In my anguish I begged for his blessing of peace, and He gave it to me, but it was in His timing and on His terms. He must get all the glory, honor and praise. I can do nothing on my own. This book, this story is His. It is His testimony, not mine.

The elements found in the Peace Equation are themes found often in the Bible. *Confidence* in God, or perhaps lack of confidence, was a problem for many Biblical figures, people who went on to become spiritual giants. James and Jude, the half-brothers of Jesus, openly mocked their sibling in John 7:3-5.

"So his brothers said to him, 'Leave here and go to Judea, that your disciples also may see the works you are doing. For no one works in secret if he seeks to be known openly. If you do these things, show yourself to the world.' For not even his brothers believed in him." James 7:3-5

Later, upon seeing the resurrected Jesus, they were confident of His divinity and became devoted followers of Christ. We know that James even gave his life for his belief.

Paul took a heavenly *perspective* when he wrote to the Philippians about his future.

"For to me to live is Christ, and to die is gain. If I am to live in the flesh, that means fruitful labor for me. Yet which I shall choose I cannot tell. I am hard pressed between the two. My desire is to depart and be with Christ, for that is far better. But to remain in the flesh is more necessary on your account." Philippians 1:21-24

Paul is telling the church members in Philippi that he is ready to die and enjoy eternity in heaven with Jesus – to die is gain. After all, he had suffered greatly for the gospel, as we know in his account in 2 Corinthians 11 – beatings, imprisonment, stoning, shipwrecks, exposure to cold, toil and hardship... his ministry was no vacation. However, he was perfectly willing to continue serving Christ here on Earth – to live in the flesh. Either way, he would be happy. His attitude was, "whatever God wants." Oh, how I wished that I had Paul's attitude all the time. I'd been ready to die when my life hit bottom. I was only thinking of my own pain and not God's will for my life. What lesson was He trying to teach me? We should all have a heavenly attitude. Of course, no rational person would want to endure the suffering Paul did, but the love and perspective of Jesus can make us act irrationally (in a good way).

There are several examples of faithful *patience* in the Bible – Noah built the ark over a period of several decades, enduring a lot of ridicule along the way. Abraham and Sarah waited 'til they were 100 and 90, respectively, before God gave them a son, Isaac. In Luke 2 we read about Simeon, who waited his entire life to see the Messiah. Joseph was sold by his brothers into slavery, was accused of sexual assault and put into prison, yet he never lost faith in God and never blamed his bros for his woes. Me? I would have been a little miffed about that. Patience is a virtue and a fruit of the Spirit. For the believer, patience is *knowing* God will provide, deliver, rescue, heal, empower and restore, but we may have to wait.

The Lord always knows the outcome, but we do not. It is often through trials and pain that our patience turns to confidence. As we mature in Christ,

138

the Holy Spirit gives us God's perspective. That's when the light bulb goes on, the Eureka! moment when the Holy Spirit gives us sanctifying faith and the peace that goes with it.

Why did I not learn this equation sooner? I think it was because I was not ready. It took a three-year struggle, added onto a lifetime of experiences, to produce within me the attitudes I needed to understand God's Peace Equation:

(Confidence = patience x time)
Faith + *Confidence* + Perspective = Peace

There is a passage in Psalms 37:3-7 that speaks to this issue of faith, patience, confidence, perspective and peace. In this passage, the author is instructing the reader to not envy evil people who prosper. However, the parallel message is that God will take care of the righteous if we put His kingdom first and wait on His timing. The emphasis and parenthetical words are mine:

"**Trust** in the Lord (confidence), and do good; dwell in the land and befriend faithfulness (patience). Delight yourself in the Lord, and he will give you **the desires of your heart** (peace).

Commit your way to the Lord; **trust in him, and he will act** (confidence). **He will bring forth your righteousness** (faith) as the light, and your justice as the noonday.

Be still before the Lord and **wait patiently** (patience and perspective) for him; fret not yourself over the one who prospers in his way, over the man who carries out evil devices!

January 7, 2012

Dear Lefty,

I was doing my daily Bible reading this morning and I happened to be in Proverbs. There are two incredibly powerful verses in Chapter 3.

"Trust in the Lord with all your heart; do not depend on your own understanding. Seek His will in all you do and He will direct your paths."

As you know, the book of Proverbs focuses on wisdom. It's fascinating to me that God tells us very clearly the value of wisdom, yet so few of us – myself included – act wisely. What exactly is wisdom? Well, it's complicated to say what "wisdom" is in a sentence or two, but He does tell us "the fear of the Lord is the beginning of wisdom." If we begin with that precept, we can build from there.

Nobody is wise all the time. I have certainly done many things that were terribly unwise. We all are human and make mistakes – God knows this and is quick to forgive. The question is, do we have the ability to learn from our mistakes? That characteristic is what separates the wise from the unwise.

I have always thought you were wise beyond your years. I still feel that way. You made some mistakes but you have recently acted very responsibly. You have stayed in treatment, listened to your counselors and read the 12-step books. Staying sober won't be easy, but you are well prepared for the fight.

This is a new beginning for you. The old life is gone and your new life is incredibly exciting. Who knows what wonderful things are in the future for Jordan Gibbs. Oh, how I wish I were 23 again. Well, not really – I'm pretty happy being 55, except my knees hurt a lot.

Only God knows how much your mother and I love you. As I've said many times before, I have prayed for you every day of your life and will continue to do so for as long as I live. Remember that if you seek His will in all you do, He will direct your paths.

Love,
Dad

Chapter 10 Stewards of a powerful testimony

"So be truly glad. There is wonderful joy ahead, even though you have to endure many trials for a little while. These trials will show that your faith is genuine. It is being tested as fire tests and purifies gold— though your faith is far more precious than mere gold. So when your faith remains strong through many trials, it will bring you much praise and glory and honor on the day when Jesus Christ is revealed to the whole world." 1 Peter 1:6-7 (NLT)

Life in the Arkansas River delta is tough. My dad and my granddad were "buckshot farmers" in Arkansas. Buckshot is the term used to describe soils with a large proportion of clay particles. When these soils dry, small round aggregates form at the surface that resemble shotgun buckshot, hence the name.[12] This type of soil is typically dark, dense and rich, perfect for rice and soybeans. It is sticky when wet and cracks open when dry. Tilling this type of soil takes strength, the strength of powerful machines and the strength of men who are willing to work very hard over a lifetime. I have friends and family who have farmed this region for many decades. They have both physical strength and strength of character that extends way down into their souls.

When viewed from ground level, the Arkansas delta is ugly and unforgiving. It is crisscrossed by stagnant swamps and ditches, cluttered by thorny underbrush, populated with a wide variety of snakes and varmints, and thick with mosquitoes and other biting and stinging insects. The entire region is flat, mostly devoid of aesthetic beauty, it floods easily and the weather is sweltering in the summer. Few would choose to live there unless their livelihood depended on it, which is why so many people over the years have chosen to leave the small towns and villages in Southeast Arkansas for a more comfortable life elsewhere.

I've traveled a great deal in my business career and have flown over the Arkansas River delta many times. It's funny how different it looks from 20,000 feet. When you look down on those buckshot farms what you see are lush green fields, glimmering streams and ribbons of blacktop roads that evoke thoughts of peaceful bucolic country living. It is beautiful. The perspective is much different when you are in rubber hip boots, standing in the middle of a rice field in August with snakes and skeeters vying for your

144

attention. It was that type of work that motivated me to go to college.

Perspective. No other factor in the Peace Equation is more difficult to grasp than perspective. Life on Earth is all we know and our view of heaven is sketchy, at best. We don't see our lives from God's perspective, we see it from the hot, sweaty, uncomfortable and sometimes dangerous ground-level view of life. Our Father knows that our trials here on Earth represent only a blip in time, but to us... well, life can seem like an eternity. Consider the emotions you feel when a loved one dies. We feel genuine pain and a deep sense of loss because it seems as though we will never see them again "this side of heaven," and from our perspective, heaven is a lifetime away.

A 10-year-old girl named Rainey Lipscomb had a wonderful perspective on life and death that she shared in a classroom essay some years ago. In response to the question, "Why do people have to die?" she wrote, "Some people take dying too seriously. It's not that sad really, if you know they have given their life to Jesus. You know that you will see them again in heaven." Wow, what profound faith from a kid! Clearly, she had a heavenly perspective.

Rainey learned much of her spiritual maturity from her parents, Cindy and Mat Lipscomb. Cindy and Mat had an unwelcome "15 minutes of fame" in 1999 when their two oldest daughters, Rainey and Lacey, were killed in an Amtrak accident in Bourbonnais, Illinois. Cindy, their three young daughters and some family friends were returning to Memphis via passenger train from Chicago after a short vacation. It was an overnight journey and the two oldest Lipscomb girls pleaded with their mom to let them share a berth with their friend, Ashley Bonnin, in one of the forward cars. Cindy relented to the traveling slumber party and the girls, ages 10 and 8, made their way to their friend's berth. About 9:30 that evening, a semi tractor-trailer rig hauling steel tried to make a late crossing in front of the train. The driver of the tractor-trailer misjudged the speed of the train and a collision ensued. The sleeper car carrying the Lipscomb daughters and their friend derailed and burst into flames. The Lipscombs' young friend survived, though she lost part of her leg. The two Lipscomb girls and nine others died in the crash.

"I got a call that evening at about 11:30 from my friend Max Bonnin, whose wife and daughter also were on the trip," said Mat Lipscomb, a successful businessman who had been a follower of Jesus Christ since he was 12 years old. Max said, 'Mat, I have horrible news. There has been a terrible accident. Ashley, my Ashley, has lost part of her leg. I have no news of any of the others!'"

There were no flights to Chicago at that hour, so Mat, Max and other family quickly arranged a two-car caravan to Illinois. With little news to go on, they headed up Interstate 55 North for the nine-hour ride. Along the way Mat received a call from a complete stranger who informed him that his wife Cindy, and youngest daughter Jesse Anne had survived the accident and were okay, but they were still searching for his older daughters. "I began to fear that something very precious to me had been lost," said Mat.

Mat was reunited with Cindy and their youngest child in Chicago as the facts surrounding the accident were revealed. Most of the blame was focused on the truck driver. Reporters covering the catastrophe were eager to get a reaction from the victims, and within hours began to approach Mat and Cindy for their response. The Lipscombs, over-whelmed with grief, were reluctant to comment, but a pastor friend, who knew well the depth of their faith, spoke to them about their responsibilities as followers of Jesus. "Tomorrow morning's newspaper may be the only Bible some people will ever read," said the pastor. "I think you ought to do the interview." Mat and Cindy prayed, then relented to speak with a reporter. "Cindy and I wanted to be good stewards of this tragedy and speaking through the media was one way we could do that. It was a way we could tell more people about Jesus than we could have ever thought possible in our lifetimes," Mat explained.

147

They told a story of forgiveness. They admitted their heartbreak and pain to the reporters, but refused to blame the truck driver. Instead, they focused on forgiveness – the forgiveness we have through Jesus Christ. They repeated this theme in all the interviews they gave in the weeks that followed. Speaking with Katie Couric on The Today Show, Mat said, "Katie, we all make mistakes every day, and so do you. We've made mistakes behind the wheel of a vehicle, but fortunately our mistakes have not crossed paths with catastrophe in the way this event has. We have forgiven the truck driver, but it's not important that he knows we forgive him. What is important is that he knows forgiveness is available from God through His son, Jesus."

According to news monitoring services, the Lipscombs were able to share their message of forgiveness with 28 million people through various interviews. What was the impact? Mat related this report: "Many weeks after the accident, Robert Hooker, a Baptist preacher and friend of ours in Chicago, wrote me to say that he had just baptized the 37th person who had been saved, in part, because of our story and how it had affected their faith in Jesus. We've heard similar stories from other ministers."

The loss of two precious young daughters was incredibly painful. "Cindy prayed for our plane to crash on the way home from Chicago because she couldn't bear the thought of returning home without the girls," admitted Mat. But faith – and confidence in God's promises – allowed the Lipscombs to see the situation from God's perspective. Rainey said it best in her essay a few weeks before she died: "(Death) is not that sad really, if you know they have given their life to Jesus. You know that you will see them again in Heaven." The Lipscombs chose to take God's perspective; their girls had simply gone ahead to their permanent home and were now awaiting the arrival of their parents and baby sister. In August, 2012, there *was* a reunion in heaven as Rainey and Lacey welcomed their mom with kisses, hugs and laughter; Cindy Lipscomb died of a brain tumor at age 58.

Fifteen years after losing his two beautiful daughters, and only two years removed from the tragic loss of his wife, Mat Lipscomb is at perfect peace with his circumstances and in his relationship with Jesus. He stays busy with his business, short-term mission trips, frequent fishing excursions and maintaining a loving and close relationship with his youngest daughter, Jesse Anne.

"There are two questions a parent always asks when they are separated from their children; where are they and who are they with? I know the answer to both questions," he responded confidently. "Knowing the answer to those questions helped us enormously, even immediately after the accident. I think the Lord granted us an uncommon peace for two reasons: the literally millions of people who heard about our story and were praying for us. We felt the power of those prayers and that was essential to our peace. Also, God had a work He wanted us to do that we could not have done if we had not been at perfect peace. We had this powerful testimony to share, and there were numerous opportunities to share it following the accident. We had to be at peace to do that, and it was not something I could have done on my own, it had to come from God."

According to Mat, the Holy Spirit was working to prepare them for the tragedy even before it occurred. "Several weeks before the wreck Cindy and I both had a premonition that something bad was going to happen, though we didn't know what. Cindy said at the time that we were two people who had never had their faith tested; nothing really bad had ever happened to us. We wondered how we would respond. For some reason I sort of assumed it would be something that would happen to me. What I realized shortly after the accident was that the Holy Spirit had been preparing our hearts for His purpose. The things that Rainey wrote in her school essay, the fact that both kids had professed faith in Jesus previously, the premonition Cindy and I had… all of this was to help us prepare for the shock we were about to experience."

Certainly, it is wonderful that people like Mat and Cindy Lipscomb could have the peace and faith necessary to proclaim Christ after such a horrendous tragedy. To God be the glory! But why would a loving Father require such a crushing sacrifice? Is this too great a price to pay?

"People have asked if following Christ is worth all of this, the loss of my girls and my wife. The short answer is, yes, it is absolutely worth it, but some explanation is necessary. I know the meaning of life; we are on this planet to learn to love God and to serve Him and accept His son Jesus as Lord and Savior, and to encourage others to do the same. Therefore, I am honored that God chose us to have this testimony. We were able to share this story, the story of God's forgiveness, with more than 28 million people. I don't like the vehicle that God chose, but I am glad that God helped us take a terrible situation and make something good from it. I can't change what happened, but I can choose how I respond to it. I want to be a witness to the love and mercy of Jesus Christ."

With such a strong faith, does Mat ever experience moments of depression or grief?

"I miss them terribly. I get surprised sometimes; I get caught off guard with a moment of grief, but I have never lost my peace. I attribute that to the prayers for us and to the reservoir of faith we had built up over several years before the accident. And who says I won't have to go through another tragedy. The thing I have to remember, the thing I must always keep in mind is that we are not here on this Earth for long. Compared to eternity, it is the blink of an eye. Until then, I have to be a good steward of this testimony."

(Since my kids were old enough to talk I have kept a list of the funny or poignant things they have said. Here is a sampling of Jordan's most memorable quotes.)

When she was two, we tried to teach Jordan to say "big girl panties" as part of her potty training. She garbled the phrase into what sounded like "goo-goo bees." Goo-goo bees became our word for underwear for the next 10 years.

At age three, she made the following comment about a sunset: "At night, God puts the sun in his pocket."

Jordan at age four: "Mustard is butter for hot dogs."

At age four she was caught eating a third cookie when she was supposed to have only two. She explained the error: "I just forgot. These cookies make me forgettable."

At age five, Jordan asked one day if she was pretty. Dad replied, "I'd rather you be pretty inside. Is your heart pretty?" Jordan said with a big grin, "Dad, my heart has stars."

Jordan's mom worked as a pharmaceutical rep for 28 years. She sometimes had to miss certain school functions. Mom was feeling guilty one time and told Jordan, "I'm sorry I couldn't be at your Easter egg hunt today." Jordan, who was six at the time, tried to cheer mom up by saying, in all sincerity, "That's okay Mom, all the other mothers were there."

At age seven Jordan was helping dad wash the family van. Suddenly she paused and very seriously asked, "Dad, if you were washing Jesus's car, would you do an extra special good job?"

Jordan at age nine discussing her plans for a family: "I think I'm gonna have five or six kids then cut it off."

Chapter 11 Applying the Peace Equation to your life

"God cannot give us a happiness and peace apart from Himself, because it is not there. There is no such thing." C.S. Lewis

John Willis does not look like a spiritual giant. For one thing, he's only about 5' 6". He also has a ponytail. I met John more than 20 years ago and he has become my good friend and confidant. I overlook the fact that he is a Yankee, raised in Boston and now living in Pennsylvania. Many of my Southern friends would never understand John, but he has taught me that followers of Jesus can be from anywhere and have unusual hairstyles. I love the guy and he has been a great blessing in my life.

John is a pastor now, but he never attended seminary. He owned a marketing and advertising company for 25 years and still dabbles in that craft. He ascended to pastorhood at a small church near Philadelphia a few years ago when God provided the opportunity. You see, John has a willing heart. So does his wife, Lee. How willing? The Willis's have 11 children and 10 are adopted. Some have special needs and many are from different ethnic backgrounds. Of the four teenagers still at home, one is Indian, one Vietnamese and two are African-American. It's like the United Nations, only less dysfunctional.

I have often called John when I've faced tough times, so he was among the first people I contacted when we discovered our daughter had an addiction problem. John is a great person to call when you are under duress because he is always so calm. He would disagree and say that he often has meltdown moments, but I've never seen one. If you've ever watched the movie *Apollo 13*, John is like the Ed Harris character, Gene Kranz. Kranz was the flight director of NASA's Mission Control who became famous for keeping cool and collected when it looked like Apollo 13 and her crew would be lost. "With all due respect, sir, I believe this is gonna be our finest hour." John has never said that to me, but it seems like something he would say. The biggest difference between John and Gene Kranz is that Kranz wore his hair in a flattop.

I asked John about his thoughts on peace that surpasses all understanding. What is it? How do you get it?

"To understand peace you have to begin from the premise that God really, really loves you. It's a personal, one-on-one love relationship, much like a loving parent has for their child." As John explains this, he begins using hand gestures to emphasize his points. "This love grows out of the love the Trinity shares for one another, and we read about this in John chapter 17, where Jesus is praying for Himself. Jesus speaks of the loving relationship that He shared with the Father and Holy Spirit before the world began. In verse 11 Jesus prays for His followers, 'Father, keep them and care for them.' In verse 24 Jesus prays, 'I want these whom you have given to me to be with me,' and in verse 25 He prays, 'I will do this so that your love for me may be in them and I in them.'

"Peace comes from knowing God; knowing that God existed in a fellowship of perfect love before the creation of the cosmos, knowing we were created out of, by and for that love. Knowing that nothing can separate us from that love. Not knowing *about* the One, but *knowing* THE ONE – our Father, our Savior and His Holy Spirit on an intimate, relational basis. Once you understand this, that God genuinely loves you, you begin to trust the heart of God and to trust His promises."

Then John made it personal.

"If I *really* understood how much God loves me, I wouldn't worry about anything."

How do we learn how much God loves us? As the old children's song goes, "Jesus loves me, this I

157

know, for the Bible tells me so." The Bible tells us exactly how much God loves us in John 3:16, "For God so loved the world that He gave His only son..." There are plenty of references to God's love in the Bible, and I've read all of them. So why was God's Word insufficient in helping me achieve unsurpassed peace? I think it's because some things have to be experienced personally before they are real to you. As a young man I studied the Himalayas. I saw photos and videos of the Himalayan range. I read the statistics – eight of the tallest mountains in the world are in Nepal, the largest being Mt. Everest at 29,029 feet. The majestic Rockies, by comparison, reach about 14,000 feet. I read about Sir Edmund Hillary and Tenzing Norgay. I thought I knew a lot about the Himalayas... but I was unprepared for how I would feel when I actually saw them in person in 1998. I was overwhelmed, speechless at the size and grandeur. God's love is like that; it's far bigger and more breath-taking when we experience it in person.

Reading about God's love in the Bible is the beginning of our knowledge, but most believers won't fully understand the depth, height and width of the Father's love until they have experienced it in their own life, and it usually takes multiple exposures to God's love before we learn to have *complete* confidence in Him. Remember: *confidence = patience x time*. This subset is essential for an understanding of unsurpassed peace. Be patient and wait on the Lord.

In time you will begin to understand how much He loves you. To have the peace that surpasses all understanding you must first be confident that God "really, really loves you."

John (my friend, not the apostle) related a story about an exercise he did in his church. He asked the congregation to write on an index card the one thing that kept them from committing their lives totally to Jesus. "I expected they would write down specific sin issues like 'greed' or 'lust,' but an overwhelming number – about 75 percent – wrote 'fear of the unknown.' They were telling me that they were not confident of God's love."

Only personal experience with God's faithfulness can help build complete confidence in God's love. As James 1:2-4 teaches,

"Dear brothers and sisters, when troubles come your way, consider it an opportunity for great joy. For you know that when your faith is tested, your endurance has a chance to grow. So let it grow, for when your endurance is fully developed, you will be perfect and complete, needing nothing." (New Living Translation)

It is hard to do so in the moment, but we should thank our Father for allowing us to endure difficult life challenges. James said it is an opportunity for great joy. This is why Paul begins his discussion of unsurpassed peace in Philippians 4 with the admonition to "rejoice in the Lord always; again I will say rejoice." Painful experiences are the gateway to a closer, more intimate relationship with Jesus. You have to have a "dark night of the soul" before you can experience God's great love. Put another way, without the dark night, there cannot be morning light. It is through these hard times that God proves His promises are true. In 2 Corinthians 4:16-18, Paul encourages the believers to remain positive during difficult times.

"So we do not lose heart. Though our outer self is wasting away, our inner self is being renewed day by day. For this light momentary affliction is preparing for us an eternal weight of glory beyond all comparison, as we look not to the things that are seen but to the things that are unseen. For the things that are seen are transient, but the things that are unseen are eternal."

An eternal weight of glory beyond all comparison! Hold on to that promise when you are in the middle of the battle. In doing so, your struggle will begin to turn to peace.

Peace is wonderful, but the peace that surpasses all understanding is something more, something better. It is more than the absence of anxiety and stress, it is peace blended with joy, it is contentment in all circumstances, even the worst you can imagine. It is happiness for what God is doing in your life and *will do* in your life because of the crisis you are now experiencing. God wants us to have this peace, an unsurpassed peace that only He can provide. See Philippians 4:4-7 for details.

How can we be happy when life is crappy? Think about childbirth. My only experience with birthing babies is as a spectator. I've been there, like a season ticket holder, watching the event from the sideline, cheering for my wife as she endured searing pain and the indignity of the delivery room. My wife is pretty tough, but she was in real agony. Even though the pain was excruciating, she was willing, even happy, to go through it because she knew something great would result. There was purpose in her pain.

What is your purpose in life? What is your desire? Our purpose and desire should reflect God's purpose and desire. We were created for God's glory. That is our purpose.

"So, whether you eat or drink, or whatever you do, do all to the glory of God." 1 Corinthians 10:31

How can we bring glory to God? We can live in such a way that our faith in God is unmistakable. We can love others as we love ourselves. We can be obedient to the Great Commission, "go therefore and make disciples of all nations, baptizing them in the name of the Father, and of the Son and of the Holy Spirit," (Matthew 28:19). If we are believers, we must be willing to sacrifice for the cause of Christ. All of these are intentional actions. We must decide to put God's glory above all else. This is often inconvenient. Sometimes it is painful.

God can use all things, all circumstances, all difficulties, even all tragedies to accomplish a very good purpose – the salvation and redemption of people. Does that thought give you peace? It can and should IF you love God with all your heart, soul and mind *and* love others as yourself. That is God's desire. Will your suffering be unpleasant? Of course it will. Will God take away all the pain, anxiety and grief? It won't disappear completely, but God will use the peace that only He possesses to guard your heart and mind in Christ Jesus.

(Confidence = patience x time)
Faith + *Confidence* + Perspective = Peace

For a long time I was confused by preachers who would say things like, "we should strive to be more and more like Jesus." My initial response to that statement was an attempt to be "more perfect;" that is, to sin less. Well, that's a noble objective, but let's face it, achieving a life of zero sin is not gonna happen, at least not for me. Too many bad thoughts, too many angry responses, too much selfishness – I just can't get there. But I now understand better what those preachers were trying to say. Our attitude, our *perspective*, about non-believers can be more like Jesus. He suffered and died for sinners. If my suffering makes me better equipped to share my faith, then I can be better equipped to accept the suffering a little better. Don't get me wrong, I don't want to suffer more to be more like Jesus. Jesus did not want to suffer, either. But if suffering does come along again, and it probably will, I pray that my perspective is like my Savior's. My pain can perhaps create a bond among Jesus, others, and me; a bond that can be used to heal and save. This helps me to better understand why Jesus had to suffer. Not only was He paying the penalty for our sins, His anguish creates unity with His followers, me included.

In his landmark book, *The Purpose Driven Life*, Pastor Rick Warren wrote, *"Other people are going to find healing in your wounds. Your greatest life messages and your most effective ministry will come out of your deepest hurts."* That quote reminds me of people like Mat Lipscomb, who lost two young daughters in a train accident but turned the tragedy into a testimony of the forgiveness of God. Or B.J. and Whitney Clay, whose daughter Callie lived only 15 hours, yet had such a profound impact on their lives and ministries. Or my sister-in-law Sherry, who endured a hellish 11 months of addiction, cancer and death, but came away thankful and blessed. Only Jesus can affect someone this way. Their stories prove that God's Peace Equation is real and that we can achieve peace that surpasses all understanding if we have faith + confidence + perspective. We must trust

God and know that He loves us like His own children and that suffering in this life is necessary for Him to develop in us faith and righteousness.

"It is for discipline that you have to endure. God is treating you as sons. For what son is there whom his father does not discipline? If you are left without discipline, in which all have participated, then you are illegitimate children and not sons... For the moment all discipline seems painful rather than pleasant, but later it yields the peaceful fruit of righteousness to those who have been trained by it. Therefore, lift your drooping hands and strengthen your weak knees..." Hebrews 12:7-8, 11-12

It should be noted that God's plan is almost never linear. You cannot simply add A + B + C to achieve D. But we can trust Him to do what is ultimately and eternally best for us. In Hebrews 4:15-16 Paul writes, *"For we do not have a high priest who is unable to sympathize with our weaknesses, but one who in every respect has been tempted as we are, yet without sin. Let us then with confidence draw near to the throne of grace, that we may receive mercy and find grace to help in time of need."* We can be confident that God <u>always</u> keeps His promises. However, how He keeps His promises is often surprising, even amazing. I have often heard the expression, "The Lord works in mysterious ways." That phrase is not found in the Bible, but there is some truth in it. The Peace Equation is not in the Bible, either. It is only a simple way to understand how a loving Heavenly Father uses the awful things that happen in life to bring us closer to Himself. If our hearts are in tune with Jesus – if our relationship with Him is strong – He can turn sadness and anxiety into genuine peace, a peace that surpasses all understanding.

August 27, 2011

Dear Lefty:

The second most embarrassing moment of my life...

It was my first year to attend the EPI Board of Director's meeting in Maine. There were about 10 of us, all from different parts of the country. I was the new guy, so there were several men I had never met before. The group included pastors, surgeons, CEOs, seminary professors, evangelists – a very high-caliber group. I was a little intimidated and felt out-of-place.

We were given Saturday afternoon off from our weekend of meetings so we could do some sight seeing. We visited the nearby town of Freeport where we were told to have fun and be back at the vehicles by 5 o'clock so we could return to our hotel. After walking around town most of the afternoon I returned to the place where we had parked two large SUVs. A couple of other guys were there, waiting and talking. I climbed into the back seat of one of the vehicles to rest.

Not long afterward, another of the guys, Jim, showed up. Jim was a businessman from Colorado, about six-feet-four and lanky. He had a perpetual smile and an uncanny ability to quote scripture. No matter what topic, it seemed, he could quote a passage

166

pertaining to the subject with the correct citation. He was an encyclopedia of Biblical knowledge.

I was slumped in the seat, languidly chewing gum, nearly asleep. Behind me, I heard Jim, rummaging around in a large drink cooler in the back of the SUV, looking for some specific type of beverage. As I sat there, I realized how tired my jaw was, chewing that gum. I was ready to toss it away, and as soon as Jim moved, I planned to throw it through the open back doors of the SUV into some tall grass nearby.

The particular drink Jim was seeking must have been very elusive, like a mongoose or a unicorn, because he seemed to take forever digging around in that cooler. Meanwhile, the gum in my mouth got heavier and heavier 'til it seemed like I was chewing rubber. Behind me, Jim continued his search, head down, intently pushing around ice and cans.

The distance from my seat in the rear of that SUV to the open back door of the vehicle was maybe two feet. The space between the top of Jim's head and the top of the roof of the SUV was about 12 inches. I reckoned there was no need to wait for Jim to move; I'd just toss the wad of gum over his head and into the grass. One lesson I have learned in life is nothing is as easy as it seems. The very millisecond I released the gum, I realized that my aim was off, perhaps only by a fraction of an inch. In the brief moment between the time it left my fingertips and the time it nicked the

SUV's roof, I died a thousand deaths. What happened next was inevitable, a perfect example of Murphy's Law.

The wad deflected onto the crown of Jim's head. Thinking an insect had landed, he exclaimed, "What's that?" and smacked the top of his head with his open palm. The gum was instantly pressed into his hair. I sat three feet away, desperately trying to think of an alibi. Maybe a plane flew over and someone tossed out their gum. Perhaps it was a bird. Aliens?

I had to man-up and admit the ugly truth. Soon I was standing behind the SUV, attempting to pick the sticky mess from Jim's (fortunately) short crop. The rest of the guys were showing up by this time, laughing hysterically at the scene and snapping photos. Jim had to shave a two-inch circle on the back of his head to remove all of the gum, making him look like a monk.

I consider myself lucky that Jim is among the most Godly and forgiving people I have ever met. The photos haunt me to this day.

Love,
Dad

Epilogue The birds are singing

It is springtime as I write this and today is a perfect day. A crabapple tree outside my window is in full bloom. I can literally hear birds chirping. My soul is totally and completely peaceful.

What's happening in our lives now? About three years ago, my daughter Jordan was informed that the restaurant where she was a waitress was closing and she would lose her job. At the time she was less than a year into sobriety, so this was worrisome news. There are few jobs available in the small town of Corinth, Mississippi, and she had a baby to support. She considered the various opportunities for work and decided to stop by the rehabilitation facility where she had most recently received treatment. As one of the largest employers in the area, maybe they would have an opening for a receptionist or kitchen worker. As God would have it, they remembered her and recalled that she had a healthcare-related degree from college and that she was very bright. They had an opening for a counseling position and they needed a qualified person for the job. Would she be interested?

My, oh my, how wonderful is God!

Jordan was delighted to have the opportunity, and not just for the paycheck. She now has a chance to help others who are struggling with addiction. In addition to working full-time at the facility, she recently completed a master's degree program in counseling (earning straight A's) and has passed her third anniversary of sobriety. She also now has two beautiful, perfect children, Tucker and Tessa – our first grandchildren. She and the children's father, who also is successfully recovering from addiction, are living happily in rural Mississippi. They recently purchased land on which to build a house. We are incredibly proud of the woman and mother she has become.

My son, Rainey, and I will go fishing tomorrow. He has more time for fishing with his old man these days since he no longer plays baseball. We always have a great time together and I consider him a friend. I'm not sure what I'll do for a fishing partner when he goes off to college. It is worth noting that he is taller than me, more handsome than me and quite a bit smarter. He was baptized last year and will be a counselor at church camp this summer. Meanwhile, our daughter Haley continues to shine light into everyone's life. She is a successful hair stylist who has twice been on local TV in recent months to demonstrate hair styling tips. She is in high demand among brides and debutantes. She is self-confident, intelligent and extremely quick-witted. It is impossible to be unhappy around her — I've tried, can't do it. She also walks with the Lord, a fact that adds to my peace.

Tracy, my wife, is simply the best person I know. You can ask anyone who knows her and they would agree. I wish I had a buck for every person that has said, "Your wife is amazing." As an unemployed writer, I could sure use the money.

Having resigned my job, I no longer have those worries to keep me up at night. Quitting your job is not something I recommend to anyone, except if God is encouraging you to do it. Only God is qualified to give that type of career advice, and leaving your job may not make your spiritual life better. I would suggest you pray long about such a decision, and if you are convinced that God wants you to make the move, go for it. As someone once said, the safest place to be is in the center of God's will. For the record, this is the second time in my career that I quit a perfectly good job because I thought God was telling me to. It worked out great the first time. And this time? So far, so good... I'm trusting God for tomorrow.

Having said that, I have no idea what God has in store for me tomorrow or next week or next year. Who knows where I will land on the board game of life (I hope its "You have won second prize in a beauty contest, collect $10"). One of the things I have always enjoyed is writing. Maybe writing for the Lord is my purpose, at least for this season of my life. I guess God really *has* given me the desires of my heart (Psalm 37:4). If His plan for me changes, I'm okay with that because I have confidence in Him based on my previous experiences, and that gives me genuine peace.

My eyes well with tears when I think of how good God is. "God is good." Christians frequently say that when something good happens in their life. But He is good even when bad stuff happens. He's good even when you are anxious or depressed. He is good no matter your circumstances. He is the provider of peace that surpasses all understanding. Remember that bumper sticker, "No God, no peace; Know God, know peace?" There is a lot of truth in that statement.

Psalm 23 is sort of a Biblical cliché. It is the one passage of Scripture most people have heard, even if they can't remember what it's about. Maybe they remember, "The Lord is my shepherd," and the part about the "valley of the shadow of death," but the rest is a muddled memory. When you write about God and His unsurpassed peace, it's hard to say anything better than Psalm 23. If you're struggling with life and faith, let me remind you of the psalmist's poem to our Heavenly Father. Read it slowly, out loud.

"The LORD is my shepherd; I shall not want.

He makes me lie down in green pastures.

He leads me beside still waters. He restores my soul.

He leads me in paths of righteousness for his name's sake.

Even though I walk through the valley of the shadow of death, I will fear no evil,

for you are with me; your rod and your staff, they comfort me.

You prepare a table before me in the presence of my enemies;

you anoint my head with oil; my cup overflows.

Surely goodness and mercy shall follow me all the days of my life,

and I shall dwell in the house of the LORD forever."

THE END

About the Author

Stephen K. Gibbs is a writer living in Memphis, Tennessee. He has a B.S. degree in public relations and an M.S. in mass communications from Arkansas State University. He and his wife Tracy have three children and two grandchildren. Steve is an elder at Central Church in Collierville, Tenn., and serves on the board of directors for two ministry organizations, Eagle Projects International and Olford Ministries International.

Bibliography

1   http://www.adaa.org/about-adaa/press-room/facts-statistics (page 5)

2   http://www.cdc.gov/mentalhealth/basics/mental-illness/depression.htm (page 6)

3   http://www.nimh.nih.gov/health/publications/anxiety-disorders/index.shtml?ct=39988 (page 6)

4   http://www.huffingtonpost.com/randy-taran/stress-and-happiness_b_3077268.html (page 6)

5   James Dobson, *When God Doesn't Make Sense* (Tyndale House Publishing page 7)

6   Howstuffworks.com/fingerprinting3.htm (page 23)

7   Ibid (page 23)

8   http://well.blogs.nytimes.com/2013/08/12/a-glut-of-antidepressants/?_php=true&_type=blogs&_r=0 (page 24)

9   http://earthobservatory.nasa.gov/IOTD/view.php?id=82550 (page 25)

10   Hank Hanegraaff, *The Prayer of Jesus*, pg 10, Thomas Nelson Publishers, 2001 (page 58)

11   http://www.nationalcathedral.org/worship/sermonTexts/bg010914.shtml (page 89)

12   http://msucares.com/crops/soils/ (page 96)

52285847R00108

Made in the USA
Lexington, KY
23 May 2016